THE MADMAN DIVINE

(El Loco Dios)
(*A Prose Drama in four acts*)
By José Echégaray

Translated from the Spanish by Elizabeth Howard West
To María Guerrero and Fernando Díaz de Mendoza

Fredonia Books
Amsterdam, The Netherlands

The Madman Divine:
El Loco Dios

by
José Echegaray

ISBN: 1-4101-0606-3

Copyright © 2004 by Fredonia Books

Fredonia Books
Amsterdam, The Netherlands
http://www.fredoniabooks.com

All rights reserved, including the right to reproduce this book, or portions thereof, in any form.

In order to make original editions of historical works available to scholars at an economical price, this facsimile of the original edition is reproduced from the best available copy and has been digitally enhanced to improve legibility, but the text remains unaltered to retain historical authenticity.

THE MADMAN DIVINE*
(El Loco Dios)
(*A Prose Drama in four acts*)
By José Echégaray
Translated from the Spanish by Elizabeth Howard West

To María Guerrero and Fernando Díaz de Mendoza

I dedicate this drama, which is more theirs than mine, on account of the artistic success which they have realized in its presentation. They are already aware, without further expression, of the enthusiastic admiration and true affection of

José Echégaray.

CHARACTERS

Fuensanta	Ramona
Gabriel de Medina	Baronesa del Romeral
Don Baltasar	Señora de Almeida
Don Leandro	First Gentleman
Don Modesto	Second Gentleman
Angeles	Doctor Torres
Doña Andrea	Restituto
Paco	Basilio
Don Esteban	Two Madhouse Attendants

ACT I

(Scene: *a fashionable summer villa near Barcelona. An elegant salon; door in the background, affording a view of a garden. Time: day.*)

Scene I

Don Baltasar, Don Modesto, and Don Leandro

Leandro.— Fuensanta is very late. She is treating us with very little ceremony; but then, that is only to be expected among kinsfolk.

Baltasar.— Kinsfolk — to be sure we are; and very near. I, for instance, am or was her father's brother,— peace to his ashes.

Modesto.— Exactly; her uncle. And an uncle is an uncle, isn't he?

Balt. (*looking at him with some degree of annoyance*).— You, Don Modesto, are also Fuensanta's uncle.

Mod.— On her mother's side.

Balt.— It must be confessed, Don Leandro, that you are related slightly to my niece, but the connection is so distant ——

Mod.— Very distant.

Lean.— But I am a good friend.

Balt.— She has invited us to spend the day with her ——

Mod.— And to dine with her; don't forget that!

Balt.— To be sure. And here we are gathering; you from Barcelona (*to* Don Leandro), Don Modesto from his villa, I from mine; Andrea will be here soon, with her son Paco; and Don Esteban will come.

Lean.— In other words, all her loving family.

Balt.— Just so. And she — she goes out for a drive without waiting for us, without so much as thinking about us. It is not right, Don Leandro, it is not right.

Lean.— Don't be so hard on her. Poor Fuensanta is very, very delicate, so her physician tells me. Her nerves, her heart ——

Balt. (*with interest which he strives to repress*).—Really? Is Fuensanta very ill? Is her nervous disorder serious?

Mod. (*with decision foreign to his character*).— Don't pay any attention to nerves; they are not necessarily fatal. The heart: that's what counts; that can bring death in five minutes. Has Fuensanta any heart trouble? (*To* Don Leandro.)

Lean.— A great deal.

Mod. (*anxiously*).— A great deal?

Balt. (*with ill-concealed excitement*).— A great deal?

Lean.— Bitterness, sadness, yearnings, charities, affections, illusions!

Balt. (*contemptuously*).— A great deal, indeed, for just one heart.

Mod.— But it is possible to live a long time, in spite of all that.

Balt. (*coldly*).— You had really frightened us.

Lean.— There is no ground for alarm, but there is reason to take precautions.

Balt.— I don't believe she has any serious trouble. Ennui, lack of appetite, spleen; she is very rich, and riches always marry at last. (*Contemptuously.*)

Mod.— I believe you; she is rich; immensely rich. (*Enviously.*)

Balt.— An income of a million francs! (*Looking upward.*)

Mod. (*protesting, speaking with passion and energy*).— Hush, man, you don't know what you are talking about! Three millions! Two hundred and fifty thousand francs a month! Twelve months, three million! Twenty-five thousand dollars every two weeks! Nearly two thousand a day! (*With growing eagerness; when money is the topic of discussion, his tone is resolute.*)

Lean.— Hardly so much; money and sanctity ——

Mod.— I know it because I know it. It hasn't been three weeks since I had to draw up an exact account of the present condition of our niece's fortune, in connection with Andrea's lawsuit against Fuensanta; and I tell you, it's what you call a colossal fortune! And firm as Gibraltar! A solid mountain of gold!

Balt. (*pensively*).— Yes, it is an enormous fortune.

Mod. (*resuming his benevolent deprecatory tone*).— Enormous.

Balt.— The suit ended at last with a compromise.

Lean.— An unjust suit; absurd, senseless.

Mod.— But dangerous.

Lean.— Certain claims upon the fortune of her brother, Don Fuensanta's deceased husband; but claims without reason.

Mod. (*gently*).— There's always a reason for asking for money.

Lean.— And still more for refusing it.

Mod.— At any rate, Doña Andrea got more than forty thousand dollars by the compromise.

Lean.— Because Fuensanta is over-generous.

Balt.— The compromise was advised by that pettifogger — that shyster lawyer. (*Contemptuously.*)

Lean.— Not so fast, Don Baltasar; Gabriel de Mendia is no pettifogger nor shyster lawyer; he is a man of the most extraordinary ability.

Scene II

The same; Don Esteban *from the rear*

Esteban.— You look as if you were quarreling. Bad! Bad! Disputes are unhygienic; the heart is over-stimulated, the blood becomes overheated, the throat becomes irritated. You can do anything in this world and still keep your equilibrium; and nothing in the world is worth the trouble of losing it. Which is my greeting to you all. You were saying —— (*Seats himself, smiling coldly.*)

Balt.— No offence intended.

Lean.— You don't know him; I do. You have made his acquaintance in connection with such prosaic and commonplace proceedings as appearing for the defence in a civil suit and preparing a compromise. I became acquainted with him when he was doing an heroic deed.

Balt.— Really!

Lean.— Yes, Señor, I first saw him in a port on the Cantabrian coast on a stormy day.

Est.— A port — a tempest — an heroic deed — I can see it now; Señor de Medina has rescued a shipwrecked mariner, fighting the angry waves with superhuman valor. (*Coldly and ironically.*) But pardon me; go on.

Lean.— Why should I. You have ridiculed what I was going to say; you are laughing here at what made us weep there. Just a moment ago I could see the shore — the sea — the furious waves — the burning felucca — the poor woman weeping, mad, despairing, imploring us for her son — I could see Gabriel approach the mother and lay his hand caressingly on her head; I could hear him say, ' Don't cry, poor woman, I'm going after the lad.' And she: ' But how? — how is it possible?' And Gabriel burst out laughing, straightened himself up, and turned into a giant before our eyes; he threw himself into the sea, then into the fire, and brought the boy away. He seemed to us more than a man, almost a god! Then he went up to the woman, caught some tears from her cheek, and said to us, ' These teardrops which moisten my fingers are worth more than all the innumerable drops of water in that sea — as immense as it is stupid '; and went away laughing. And here it is, you have been laughing too.

Balt.— That's not half bad.

Est.— How are the mighty fallen! From walking amid waves and tempests to spending your days among writs, appeals, and briefs — a far cry!

Lean.— In the matter of doing good and enforcing justice modest and unobtrusive work is quite as effective as spectacular performances.

Mod.— You are not talking about me, I suppose (*smiling*), when you say modest?

Lean.— No, I'm not talking about you, Don Modesto.

Est.— At any rate, you must surely agree with me that if the figure of Gabriel among the foaming waves and the flames of the burning felucca is a noble one it loses something of its epic grandeur when it appears in a business suit or a frock coat, presenting to Fuensanta the bill for his services in the case. (*With cold irony.*)

Lean.— Always the ridiculous. We don't know whether he will present the bill you are speaking of. Gabriel used to be rich, and he still has enough to live on.

Balt.— He used to be very rich, but spent his fortune in fads and follies, didn't he?

Lean.— No, Señor. He spent his fortune in travel — he has been all over the world; in studies and experiments — he is a scholar; in works of charity — he is a philanthropist; in a word, a great intellect, a great heart, an indomitable will.

Est.— These freaks, these unbalanced geniuses either end in a madhouse or suddenly turn prudent and marry a millionairess.

Balt.— What? (*Unable to repress a certain alarm.*)

Mod.— What? Do you think so? (*Dropping his suave tone; whenever money is under discussion he changes completely.*)

Est.— He wouldn't be the first lawyer who took a marriage settlement in lieu of a fee.

Balt.— It would be an indignity.

Mod.— It would be a disgrace.

Est.— It would be a mighty fine thing for Gabriel, but it would be a piece of great imprudence on Fuensanta's part. I know that her health is very delicate.

Lean. (*drily*).— You have consulted the doctor, too, about the probabilities in your dear niece's case!

Est.— Why not, pray? Does my interest strike you as being anything out of the ordinary?

Lean.— On the contrary, it impresses me as being very natural.

Balt.— These fears of Don Esteban's are ill founded. Fuensanta has had many admirers, and she has refused them all.

Mod.— Because she has insight enough to realize that all of them have more desire for her money than for her love.

Lean.— And in any case she has her relatives to advise her.

Est.— Of course. Really, people have slandered us.

Lean.— Slandered you?

Est.— As poor Fuensanta has always been very delicate, there are people who suppose that we are preventing her marriage. Do you understand?

Mod.— In the expectation of a speedy inheritance in the future. Just imagine our —— Poor child!

Balt.— That's enough, gentlemen. All this stuff makes me sick.

Lean.— Right you are. (*Pauses.*)

Mod.— I believe that's Doña Andrea with my Angeles.

Balt.— A beautiful state of things; we shall all have come, and no sight of Fuensanta yet. As she is giving us this dinner to celebrate her reconciliation with her deceased husband's family, it seems to me that she ought to be here to receive Doña Andrea. What a baby! good Lord, what a baby!

Est.— You are decidedly in a bad humor, Don Baltasar.

Mod.— We all are.

Scene III
The same. Doña Andrea, Angeles

Andrea.— Gentlemen. (*All bow.*) Don Modesto, I give you back your daughter safe and sound.

Angeles.— Papa! (*To* Don Modesto.)

Mod.— Sweetheart! (*All greet* Doña Andrea.) You've had a pleasant time?

Ang.— No, indeed. I'd rather spend the afternoon with Fuensanta than with Doña Andrea and her son. (*To her father in a low tone.*)

Mod.— Speak softly; don't let them hear you.

Ang.— They are not a bit nice, and they say things ——

Mod.— For heaven's sake, daughter ——

Balt.— You needn't deny it; you are out of sorts. (*To* Doña Andrea.)

And.— Well, I don't deny it; I am out of sorts. (*They gather about full of curiosity.*)

Est.— Why?

And.— I am very fond of Fuensanta; although her treatment of me leaves much to be desired, I am exccedingly fond of her. And my son, my poor Paco? My poor boy! But we'll not talk of him. And certainly Fuensanta is very imprudent, very thoughtless. What do you suppose she did to-day? Went to drive in an open calash with that lawyer! — the one who sacrificed me so inhumanly.

Mod.— And everybody saw them, I suppose.

And.— Without a doubt. When I came in, I quickened my pace so as not to meet them. Poor Paco went to receive them; they are probably in the garden by now.

Ang.— Why, they seemed to me a perfectly lovely couple. She's divine; he — oh, well, he's an — I don't know what. In a word, Gabriel awes and attracts at the same time, and he scares you a tiny bit; but it's such a pleasant kind of fear — Oh, dear, I don't know how to express myself!

Mod.— Keep still, child, you don't understand these things.

Ang.— I say what I think. (*All have sat in pensive silence since hearing* Doña Andrea; *now they break up into groups.*)

Balt. (*to* Doña Andrea).— You believe that Fuensanta has taken a fancy to this intriguer?

And.— I am afraid she has. He is a knave, and a fool to boot.

Mod.— Poor Fuensanta has not very sound judgment.

And.— Well, then, it shall not be, it shall not be; that's what we are here for.

Mod.— Trust you for that! (*This conversation has been confined to the three; they now walk to and fro through the room.*)

Ang. (*to* Don Leandro).— Why are they in a bad humor?

Lean.— Are they in a bad humor? I hadn't noticed it.

Ang.— Yes, Señor, they are. They are preoccupied; they are talking in a low tone; they are looking around suspiciously. And what faces! Whether you believe it or not, I know what I'm talking about. Once I asked papa for some money to buy me a hat, and he wouldn't give it to me: I didn't like it a bit; I was perfectly furious. Well, I went to the mirror, and my face scared me! How ugly! It looked like the face of a bird of prey; just as if I were on the point of swooping down. When I confessed this sin, the confessor told me that it was the face of vanity, of anger, and of avarice. Well, they all have that expression; their noses are curved; their mouths recede, their eyes flash; how ugly they are! But not papa; no, I'm not talking about papa!

Lean.— You are very good, but you are hypercritical, and a little malicious.

Ang.— But I know whereof I speak, Don Leandro. Leaving papa out, I fairly detest them all.

Lean. (*with comic resolution*).— Ugh! So do I!

Ang.— And we like each other.

Lean.— Immensely. (*Both laughing.*)

Scene IV

The same; Paco *from the rear*

Paco.— How do you do, gentlemen!

And.— And Fuensanta?

Paco.— In the garden with Señor de Medina. They were talking about our lawsuit.

Balt.— But why doesn't Fuensanta come in? Alone in the garden with Señor de Medina ——

And.— Did you speak to her?

Paco.— Yes.

And.— Then she knows that we are waiting for her, and still she's in no hurry to come in. Ingrate!

Paco.— We matter precious little to Fuensanta!

Ang.— I don't like this one, either; he's an everlasting nuisance.

Lean.— I don't like him either.

Ang.— Then we'll keep on being friends.

Lean.— Better and better every time.

Paco.— When Fuensanta grows tired of Gabriel's silliness and rudeness, she will come in.

Lean. (to ANGELES).— I'm going to wring that puppy's neck for him.

Est.— Why, was Gabriel rude to Fuensanta?

Paco.— Yes, Señor, he was, was positively impertinent.

Balt.— In your presence?

Paco.— Yes, Señor.

And.— And you allowed it?

Paco.— I gave him the rebuke he deserved.

Est. (mockingly).— With spirit, of course.

Paco.— I think so.

And.— What did you say?

Paco.— A cruel thing.

Balt.— Let's hear it.

Paco.— I said sternly, ' Señor de Medina, Fuensanta is Fuensanta.'

Mod.— What else?

Paco.— Don't you think that was enough? Well, he understood me; he changed countenance, and, to hide his confusion, burst out laughing.

And.— And Fuensanta?

Paco.— She wished to hide her feelings, too, because it was an awkward situation for all of us.

Lean.— And she burst out laughing too?

Paco.— Exactly. What would you have done if you had been there?

Lean.— The same thing; I'd have laughed myself.

Ang.— So would I.

Paco.— Mamma, it looks to me as if Don Leandro and Angeles were laughing.

And.— Your wit must have pleased them; you have some happy thoughts!

Paco.— Mamma, I suspect that Fuensanta doesn't like me.

And.— Oh, she'll like you in time! Why, here she is now!

Scene V

The same. Fuensanta, *from the rear*

Fuensanta.— Just as I feared! All here before me! But you'll be so good as to forgive me, won't you? You forgive me? (*Giving her hand to the nearest.*)

Paco (*approaching and offering his hand*).— Fuensanta ——

Fuen. (*without taking his hand*).— I spoke to you before. (*Looking toward* Andrea.) My dear Andrea, are you angry with me? Give me a kiss, dear lady.

And.— You are the one to forgive me. It was not my wish — but I am poor — I have a son. Nevertheless, I am disinterested. Besides, you know by this time what these lawyers are — these procurators; in a word, they upset me completely.

Fuen.— Let's drop the subject — an ancient tale forgotten. And if you are not satisfied, your wish shall be granted.

And.— For heaven's sake, Fuensanta! Don't make rash promises; I want nothing — nothing for myself; if you can kindly do something for my Paco — if he can be included in the compromise — and if you don't think best — it's all over — it's all over — the forty thousand dollars, or thereabout.

Fuen.— Good gracious! What are you talking about? I shall talk it over with Señor de Medina; I gave him a hint before — in our drive. But these lawyers — (*laughing*) law and property rights — what do I care for all that?

Balt.— Did you take a drive together?

Fuen.— Yes, we went as far as Barcelona.

Mod.— And Gabriel's conversation: do you find it interesting?

Fuen.— How do I know? He is interesting; yes, he really is. What a queer man he is! (*Pensively.*)

Est.— You find him agreeable?

Fuen.— I don't know. Sometimes he seems so; then, again, he frightens me. He is a mystery: a genuine mystery. (*All the relatives look at one another and smile.*)

Balt.— To me he seems not in the least mysterious.

And. (*in a low tone*).— He is a rascal.

Fuen.— Not at all. They tell stories of heroic deeds he has done.

Mod.— Yes, your friend Don Leandro tells them.

Lean.— Everybody knows about them.

Fuen.— He is a singular man; he seems not in the least like other men.

Years ago I took a trip through the Alpujarras. What rocks! What mountains! What untamed, magnificent nature! Sometimes you are filled with admiration; your soul yearns to leave the body and soar among those immensities of stone, those giant stairways leading up to heaven! Then, again, you are afraid; you realize that you are nothing, and the abysms of darkness are luring you. Well, I feel somewhat like that when I am near Señor de Medina. Gabriel horrifies, allures, frightens. But I don't express myself adequately. He is what I have said, certainly; but he is something else besides. Imagine that in the Alpujarras, that chaos of stone I have been speaking of, one rock should suddenly take the shape of a grotesque monster, another should change into an ape and make faces at me, a gigantic mottled ridge into a crawling reptile, a twisted, treelike projection on the edge of a precipice into a serpent coiling about me, so that the grotesque and the sublime are mingled — creatures that aspire to soar and those which grovel in the dust: the caresses of a blue sky and the brutalities of rocks and boulders. In a word, I don't know — I don't know — all that changeling nature which attracts and repels, which consoles and hurts, and finally maddens you, because thought is lost, and the heart, between shrinking and expanding, is broken. (*Falls upon the sofa, gasping for breath.*)

And.— What is the matter, Fuensanta?

Balt.— Are you ill?

Mod.— Is it your heart?

Fuen.— Yes, my heart — palpitation — but it's nothing — don't be alarmed. The same old story — it will be over in a minute.

Lean.— Are you getting better?

Fuen.— I think so. (*Trying to smile.*)

Paco.— Heart troubles are contagious. (*Laying his hand on his breast.*)

Fuen.— Well, then, don't you come near me. (*Motioning him away with her hand.*)

Ang.— Are you better?

Fuen.— Yes, it's gone now.

And. (*confidentially*).— This Don Gabriel de Medina is very dangerous; believe me, who have had experience; very dangerous!

Lean.— Now they are beginning to slander Gabriel. I can't sit here and listen to them. Let's go out on the terrace, Angeles.

Ang.— Yes, let's do; we'll feel better alone. We'll let them talk unkindly about the poor fellow; when they are gone, we'll come back and speak well of our friend.

Lean.— Good. (*The two withdraw toward the rear; the rest gather about* FUENSANTA.)

Fuen.— No; I tell you, no, Andrea. Gabriel is a very peculiar man, I don't deny that. He is very learned, has studied a great deal, and has so many ideas in his head that they roll over one another; and the result is a being who to us Philistines is incomprehensible and extravagant. But he is very high souled, very noble; indeed he is.

Balt.— You are very innocent, Fuensanta. You are very unsophisticated! I don't know how to say things in diplomatic terms; I am at times brutally frank; and I tell you with brutal frankness that Gabriel seems to me a grand fake.

Fuen.— Merciful heavens, Don Baltasar! You are unjust!

Est.— I'll not say fake. You are right, my child, it is a very harsh term. Gabriel is a good comedian; he affects admirably the eccentricities of the man of genius. Let's applaud him, all of us; but nothing more; and when the comedy is over, send him away.

Fuen.— No, Gabriel does not play a part; his intelligence may be chaotic, his heart may be uncontrolled, but he means what he says. He is a gentleman — and a superior being ——

And.— Superior! Oh, how he is deceiving you.

Paco.— Fuensanta, my dear, stop a minute and consider. If, as mamma says, Gabriel is deceiving you —— Ah! Then Gabriel is a deceiver! (*With the air of having said something profound.*)

Mod.— To be sure; there's no discounting that.

Fuen.— You'll make me nervous if you keep on!

Paco.— Oh, no; nervous troubles ——

Fuen.— Are contagious too? Then get away from me! (*Somewhat mockingly.*)

Paco.— It means so much to me. (*With exaggerated tenderness.*)

And. (*to* DON MODESTO *in a low tone*).— How clever he is!

Mod.— He's a real jewel, this chap is.

Fuen.— But, Señor, what purpose would Señor de Medina have in pretending everything he says? Why should he take the trouble to represent a comedy which, even though it is interesting at times, and even sublime, at other times is ridiculous and grotesque? With what object?

Balt.— Because he is an adventurer, and wants your money, and has made up his mind that you are to be his wife. Do you want it any plainer?

Fuen.— For the love of heaven! What an idea! Stop, for mercy's sake!

Balt.— Before declaring himself, he wants to get you tamed, hallucinated, conquered.

Fuen.— But he treats me with indifference, discourtesy, brutality, rather than affection.

Mod.— He is sly!

Est.— He's foxy!

Balt.— He knows what he's doing!

And.— How is that? (*Some look at others, smiling.*)

Fuen.— But, I tell you, it is impossible. Just now, when we were walking in the garden, a lovely butterfly fluttered before me, and I instinctively tried to catch it with the parasol I was carrying; I was awkward, and hurt the poor little creature so that it fell upon the ground. How Gabriel raved! How he abused me! I think he called me a wretch! Say, Paco, didn't he call me a wretch?

Paco.— Yes, he did, and I ——

Fuen.— Advanced to my rescue: 'Fuensanta is Fuensanta!' (*Laughing.*) Thank you very much, Paco. In a word, the lover, as you suppose, scolded me roundly. I was vexed and confused; I didn't know how to answer — whether to treat it as a joke or take it seriously; I felt my face burning; I dropped my head and walked on without saying a word. To hide my agitation I turned to pick a rose. (*Laughing.*) I couldn't have conceived a worse crime! Before I could pull it from the stem, he caught me by the wrist and said to me in an angry tone, as if I had been his daughter or he my teacher, 'Flowers are not to be pulled! Leave that rose alone!' (*Laughing.*)

And.— And you permitted it!

Balt.— Fuensanta!

Est.— Good Lord, have we come to this!

Fuen.— But he didn't give me time for anything. His eyes scared me; Oh, he looked to me like — I don't know what!

Est.— An archangel, of course.

Mod.— The archangel Gabriel!

Fuen.— I don't know — I don't know — (*Confused.*) Before I could say a word he caught hold of my hand and gave me a kiss — on the hand, wasn't it? — no, on the wrist that he had clutched before.

And.— Heavens! A kiss!

Balt.— Insolent!

Mod.— Ah! (*All look black at the idea of* GABRIEL'S *having kissed her, and some look at their own wrists.*)

Paco.— I was not there — you'd better believe I wasn't!

Fuen. (laughing).— Yes; you'd have said, 'Fuensanta's wrist is Fuensanta's'; I know you would.

Paco.— Something more, perhaps.

Fuen.— Very well, then; breaking in before I could say a word, he began to make some very singular remarks in a very gentle tone: 'Fuensanta, you are very good; don't hurt the flowers, for they don't deserve it; looking at them, admiring them, inhaling their fragrance, tenderly cherishing them, are all very well; but pulling them, pulling them, no! separating them from their stems — don't think of it! No, Fuensanta, flowers have life, my child *(laughing)*; their sap is their blood, their fragrance their breath; and breaking them from their stems kills them; it is a cruelty, a crime! Believe me, in God's name, believe me!' And he pressed my hand affectionately.

And.— Ah! How shocking! *(All grow indignant.* PACO *clenches his fists.)*

Fuen.— I began to say in a submissive tone, 'I was going to put it on my breast —' 'On your breast! the mangled rose on your breast! What would you say, you blind creature, if a powerful being, a superior, I, for example, should come into a parlor blazing with light and full of beautiful women,— blondes, brunettes,— with their elaborate coiffures, with their supple necks bare; and at the sight of these human flowers palpitating with light, with fragrance, with smiles, I should say to myself, 'Very pretty, very pretty — I want them — I'm going to pull a few;' and whack; I should cut a pretty neck and pull off a little head; and whack! I should cut another and another — and another — and making a lovely bleeding bouquet, I should put it in the buttonhole of my superior-being dresscoat? Eh? What would you say, Fuensanta?'—'I should say,' I replied, 'that you were a savage and a monster.' 'Well, that's what I think of you when you pull flowers,' he answered me with perfect composure; then he respectfully bade me good by and went away.

Balt.— Do you want any further proof of what I told you a moment ago?

And.— This makes him out no more than a knave or a fool. *(All surround her solicitously and affectionately, as if to free her from a great danger.)*

Balt.— A rascal who has learned your character and wants to dominate your imagination.

Mod.— Hypnotize you — that's what he wants to do.

And.— No, my child, don't let yourself be deceived. Pay him his fee and let him go.

Balt.— And in any case here are we.

Paco.— Here am I.

And.— Here is Paquito.

Fuen.— Yes, I see him.

Mod.— All, all of us are here. (*With solicitude, with concern, moving about her.*)

Est.— And here he is, too. (*In a low tone, and pointing toward the rear, where* GABRIEL *has presented himself, and is pausing a moment. Behind him enter* DON LEANDRO *and* ANGELES. *All move away from* FUENSANTA, *except* ANDREA, *who continues talking to her.*)

SCENE VI

FUENSANTA, DOÑA ANDREA, ANGELES, DON LEANDRO, DON BALTASAR, DON ESTEBAN, DON MODESTO, *and* PACO, *with* GABRIEL, *stockstill in the rear*

Gab. (*in a gentle, humble tone*).— Fuensanta. (*She pretends not to hear him, and continues talking with* ANDREA.)

Balt.— How familiarly he treats her! Don't you hear him? (*To* DON ESTEBAN.)

Gab. (*as before*).— Fuensanta ——

Est.— To be sure. To be sure. (*To* DON BALTASAR.)

Gab.— Fuensanta, aren't you going to answer me? Are you angry with me?

Fuen. (*turning*).— Ah! Pardon me. Did you speak? (*Coldly.*)

Gab.— Are you still angry with me?

Fuen.— I? I don't understand — What about? (*With exaggerated coolness and politeness.*)

Gab.— Down there in the garden, when we were walking together, it seems to me that I said something impolite. I don't know what, I don't remember; but I have a vague impression that I spoke to you in a stern tone.

Fuen.— Ah! You don't remember. Then I'm sure I don't. Small matter. (GABRIEL *remains pensive.*)

Balt.— The insolence of him!

Mod.— Rather — rather insolent; certainly.

Paco.— He is intolerable.

Gab.— Forgive me, Fuensanta.

Fuen.— I don't know what for,— but at any rate — if you insist upon it — you are forgiven.

Gab.— Thank you. (*Turning to the rest.*) It's a great thing,— forgiveness,— gentlemen. (*Changing his tone.*) When I forgive I feel a joy as great — as great — This is why God never tires of forgiving; He wearies not, you may rest assured.

Est.— We have no doubt of it.

Gab.— They used to say, 'Vengeance is the pleasure of the gods,'— of the gods, mind you. To-day we say, and I say, Forgiveness is the daily food, not of the gods, but of God; of the One; do you understand?

Mod.— Yes, yes, we understand.

Gab.— It looks to me as if you didn't fully comprehend; you have not the appearance of understanding me. (*To* Don Baltasar.)

Balt.— It is not so difficult — what you are saying — as to be outside the range of our intellects, however modest they may be!

Gab.— Not of your intellect, but perhaps of your will.

Est.— Now we really don't understand you.

Gab.— But I understand myself. (*Pauses.*) And forgiveness must never be abused. There are miserable beings, there are wretched beings, who must be punished, and punished severely. Just a little while ago Fuensanta hurt a poor butterfly. Ah! Now I recollect; it was that I scolded you for — he fell to the ground with one wing broken. When a butterfly's wing is broken, he falls; when a human creature is tortured by malevolent beings, and his illusions are broken, he also falls. Manifestly, with illusions he flies; when they fail him — to the ground! Well, when I came back to the place where the poor little beast had fallen, there it was, fluttering about, struggling, beating the ground with the only wing he had left, but it could not rise — could not soar into space! And a swarm of beetles, grubs, black, repulsive vermin, were surrounding the poor creature, ready to devour it! and I — I trampled them — trampled them underfoot — ground them into clay, dust, nothing! Punishment! Punishment! Punishment is also a joy! For punishment is the destruction of evil; and evil is to be destroyed unceasingly, without compunction, without mercy! Ah! If I were God! (*with growing violence.*) He is too merciful! (*In a low tone, as if he were telling a secret.*) If He could have a fault, it is this: He is too merciful.

Est. (*to* Don Baltasar).— I believe he's gone mad.

Balt. (*to* Don Esteban).— Comedy! Comedy!

Fuen. (*to* Doña Andrea).— He says clever things, you can't deny that.

And. (*to* Fuensanta).— Oh, but he doesn't mean anything, anything he says; it's all a farce!

Fuen. (*in a low, cold tone*).— And you really mean everything you say?

Gab.— If I really say it!

Balt.— Fuensanta's question is very much to the point, for at times it is very hard to distinguish truth from falsehood.

Gab.— But what do you know about truth and falsehood? Falsehood!

There are lies that are soul-stirring, sublime; and there are truths that are gloomy and depressing! (*With growing violence.*) If you work up the statistics, you will find that humanity has made more progress through great lies than through petty truths! The fact is, that a lie, as I said before, if it is very fine, very great, becomes a truth; and what a divine transformation! And a truth, if it is petty, miserable, ugly, through some miraculous transformation becomes a lie. Therefore the test is, not whether a thing is true or false, for that means nothing, but whether it is good or bad, petty or great, ugly or beautiful, repulsive or inspiring. Be it what it may, so it be good, great, beautiful, sublime, I'll throw in the truth to boot!

Fuen.— This man gives you something to think about, you can't deny that. (*To* ANDREA.)

And.— Ah! My child, how he fascinates you!

Paco (*to* DON BALTASAR).— What an actor!

Gab.— Very well; now why are we saying all this?

Mod.— I don't know.

Gab.— You don't know anything; there's reason for your being modest. (*Laughing.*) The fact is, that I came to say something to Fuensanta.

Paco (*coming forward*).— About the lawsuit? (FUENSANTA *approaches the two.*)

Gab.— No — yes — that's all very well. Listen, Doña Andrea, come here. (PACO *and* ANDREA *approach;* FUENSANTA *moves away.*) Do you want me to tell you a very great truth? I'll not say beautiful, but great, assuredly!

And.— Let's have it!

Gab.— Then all of you are in my way just now, and you two especially; isn't that so?

And.— Thank you, very much.

Gab.— Not at all. Listen. I want to talk to Fuensanta to see if she can add fifteen or twenty thousand dollars to the forty thousand of the compromise, for Paco. What do you think of that? (*Affecting a drawl.*)

And.— Señor de Medina! (*Greatly pleased.*)

Gab.— I am going away within an hour, and I should like to settle the matter fully before I go. Eh? (*With somewhat mocking maliciousness.*)

Paco.— But must you trouble yourself for us?

And.— We have said nothing ——

Gab.— I know that very well; that is just the reason why I should like to be alone with her. And these people ought to go too. For, to tell you the truth, I don't trust them any too well.

And.— Maybe you are right.

Paco.— Perhaps so. (*Giving him his hand.*) Señor de Medina is Señor de Medina.

Gab.— Thank you, Paquito. (*In a deep tone.*) They believe that Fuensanta is mortally ill, and they are sniffing at the estate; everything that involves diminishing the principal pains and disgusts them.

And.— Maybe so.

Paco.— I don't deny it. Human avarice is great avarice.

Gab.— Whereupon —— (*Showing them the door.*)

And.— In a moment.

Gab.— And take away all the people you can.

Paco.— Trust me for that!

And. (*approaching* FUENSANTA).— With your permission, dear, Paco and I are going to see the garden and the park. It's two years (*feigning sadness*) since we walked there as we used to, through its groves and bowers; and they say it is divine!

Fuen. (*preparing to accompany them*).— Yes; a good idea.

And. (*holding her back*).— No, my child, you would tire yourself. Don Leandro and Angeles will go with us. (DON LEANDRO *and* ANGELES, *who have been in the background, come forward.*)

Ang.— Certainly I will; with great pleasure.

Lean.— I am at your service.

And.— Well, then, let's go. Au revoir! Don't forget us. (*To* GABRIEL; *he bows.*)

Ang.— Come, come — you shall see -- it is a paradise.

Paco.— Ah! Paradise is nearer! (*Exeunt* DOÑA ANDREA, ANGELES, PACO, *and* DON LEANDRO.)

SCENE VII

FUENSANTA, GABRIEL, DON BALTASAR, DON ESTEBAN, DON MODESTO.
GABRIEL *takes* DON MODESTO *aside; the rest form groups, talk, promenade, etc.*

Gab.— Just a word or two, Don Modesto, my friend.

Mod.— As many as you wish.

Gab.— No, very few. Because I've already got rid of the ones who are gone, and now I'd like to get rid of you.

Mod.— Get rid of me? Am I in your way?

Gab.— Well, if you were not in my way should I be capable of depriving myself of your interesting presence?

Mod.— I think not.

Gab.— Then it is lamentable fact, but a positive one, that you are in my way.

Mod.— Very well, then, in that case —— (*Humbly; preparing to leave.*)

Gab.— Your amiability makes you worthy of my confidence. Don Modesto, within an hour I am going away.

Mod.— You are going away? (*Unable to repress his delight.*)

Gab.— Don't be ungracious; you are glad to have me — disappear.

Mod.— I assure you — Good Lord! — to think that I — Don Baltasar and Don Esteban, certainly; they dislike you intensely; but I, I — I have always said that you are a perfect gentleman, a man of great ability, and a very, very agreeable person.

Gab.— Thank you a thousand times, my dearest friend.

Mod.— Are you going very far?

Gab.— Very far.

Mod.— For a long time?

Gab.— Who knows? The future is a mystery, the past another mystery — and the present — the present is nothing at all. Therefore, I should like to say good by to Fuensanta alone — to finish the business of the lawsuit.

Mod.— Good; very good. (*He probably wants to present his bill.*) Magnificent. (*Thank the Lord he's going.*) Then I'll leave you two, and I'll take Don Esteban. I'm afraid to tackle Don Baltasar; he's awfully touchy.

Gab.— I'll attend to him.

Mod.— Don Esteban, permit me; we have something to talk about ——

Est.— With great pleasure.

Mod.— Au revoir, Fuensanta; we are going to the garden, too.

Fuen.— The house is yours — absolute freedom till dinner-time.

Mod. (*approaching* Don Esteban).— Good news! he's going away! Oh, he's a great one, is Señor de Medina!

Est.— Indeed? So much the better. (*Exeunt both.*)

Scene VIII

Fuensanta, Gabriel, *and* Don Baltasar

Gab. (*to* Fuensanta).— With your permission, I should like to say something very interesting to Don Baltasar.

Fuen.— To Don Baltasar too! You seem to have secrets with everybody! (*Withdraws to the rear.*)

Gab.— And with you, too. Your turn will come presently.
Balt.— You had something to say to me?
Gab. (*in a stern tone*).— Yes, Señor; what I said to those who are gone away.
Balt.— And what did you say to them?
Gab.— That I wanted to talk to Fuensanta; that they were in my way and must leave.
Balt.— Señor!
Gab.— To the rest of them, as they were inoffensive up to a certain point — only up to a certain point — I spoke in a mild tone; in a friendly, affectionate way; but your case is different. You have the reputation of being a hard character, a violent, hectoring bully. In a word, I dislike you intensely, and there is no reason why I should pretend what I don't feel. Try, therefore, to please me; it seems to me that I've said this politely enough.
Balt.— I brook neither threats nor impositions. You shall make me an apology! (*All this in a ringing tone, but so low that* FUENSANTA *does not hear what he says.*)
Gab.— An apology! Why, you are out of your senses! I have just told you that I detest you thoroughly, and here you are trying to make me apologize! In that case, I insult you!
Balt.— Señor de Medina!
Gab.— Yes, Señor, as great an insult as I can offer! I am a prophet! The divine spirit inspires me sometimes! Oh, I know it, I know it, and you shall be convinced! You shall reckon with me! (*With deep anger.*)
Balt.— I don't want to make a scene in Fuensanta's presence; but we shall talk about it presently. I'll look you up.
Gab.— Well, then, you'll have to be quick about it, because I'm going to Barcelona within an hour; within two hours I sail for America; and the Lord knows when we shall see each other again.
Balt.— Ah! You are going — forever. You are an original man! (*Moves away, laughing.*)
Gab.— And in gratitude for the news you forgive me the insult, do you?
Balt.— I never forgive.
Gab.— I do, sometimes, because I am that I am; but it is not easy to forgive you.
Balt.— I believe she is right; you are not very sane. (*To* FUENSANTA). I leave you with Señor de Medina. (*In a low tone.*) Either way, mad or sane, he is exceedingly dangerous. Take care, Fuensanta, take care. (*Exit.*)
Gab. (*in a low tone to* FUENSANTA).— Now we are alone.

Scene IX

FUENSANTA *and* GABRIEL. GABRIEL *drops into an armchair and keeps on in an absent-minded fashion mechanically repeating the same expression.*

Gab.— Now we are alone. Yes — now we are alone.

Fuen. (standing and looking curiously at him. Aside).— What an extraordinary man! He is interesting, immensely interesting. What is my feeling toward him? I don't know. Love, curiosity, fear, all at once? Who knows? Certainly now we are alone. (*He looks at her without rising; she impatiently draws nearer.*)

Gab.— It's true. Now they are all gone.

Fuen.— Did you wish to speak to me?

Gab.— I wanted to be alone with you.

Fuen.— To tell me something, no doubt?

Gab.— To be alone. To gaze at you — to admire you — to adore you — but alone, without having my adoration profaned by the presence of strangers, vulgar creatures, perhaps infamous. As a child I used to fly into a rage if I were in my mother's arms and some one dared come and break in upon her caresses. As a man, what a blind fury took possession of me if I were reading some work of the immortals, and some friend came in to interrupt my reading? When I am listening to divine music, the prose of life with its strident noises drives me mad. When I am looking at you, the rest of the universe is in my way; it troubles me, infuriates me; it is a noise which breaks the harmony; ugliness which mars the beauty; the mocking demon, more ape than devil, who takes his stand between me and the cross, and hides it from me. Out! Out! Out with the low, the impure, the ignoble; let them leave me with my adoration and my happiness!

Fuen. (laughing heartily).— A declaration in epic style! Sublime! Worthy of you! How much poetry monsieur the lawyer was holding in reserve for me!

Gab. (rising at this moment, or when it seems opportune).— Ridicule! This is not worthy of you! Ridicule! Weapon forbidden! The only sentiment of which the wicked and the imbecile are capable! Ridicule does not come from above, from the supreme goodness, nor from below, from the supreme evil. Satan is not ridiculous; he is great with the grandeur of evil: I forbid you to make use of ridicule against me.

Fuen.— I do not know what right you have to forbid me anything. But I accept the prohibition, and I shall speak seriously. Señor de Medina, I have my doubts of you. And doubt grieves me, because I should like to respect you, and I don't know whether you are worthy of my respect.

Gab.— Doubt, yes. It is sad; it is horrible; it is painful; but it is tragic, it is grand. Yes, it is grand; you may doubt; you have my permission to doubt.

Fuen.— It's you. I'm talking about doubting you.

Gab.— Yes, me. I am worth the trouble. There are people who doubt God!

Fuen.— Señor de Medina, I shall be frank; I shall tell you what I have told no one else in this world: in fact, good or evil, traitor or loyal, you are worth the trouble — of love or hate.

Gab.— We are of the same opinion.

Fuen.— I doubt you, because I am beginning to doubt myself. I was married, or they married me, at seventeen, to a man of seventy, because he was enormously rich; and this wealth in my possession he left me at his death. Therefore I am an unworthy creature; I sold myself, and I am enjoying the price of the infamous bargain. For I married without love; I didn't know what love was. That is why I tell you I doubt myself. How, then, can I believe in other people? If I believed in you, I should be your slave. But if I doubt you, I shall send you out of my house. So far as money is concerned, what I acquired when almost a child is enough; so far as a feeling of contempt is concerned, what I feel for myself is enough; I don't want to feel it for the man I love. Defend yourself, convince me, or else go away forever.

Gab.— Ah! This is what I thought you were! This is what I adore you for! What joy!

Fuen.— But this is not defending yourself, nor is it convincing me.

Gab.— All in good time.

Fuen.— This is representing a comedy, and always having a retort ready, but nothing else.

Gab.— This is loving you as no one else could. (*In a low tone.*) You might look for celestial beings, and on your knees you might plead with them, ' Love me as Gabriel loves me,' and they could not. Divine being, fragile creature, spirit trembling at the touch of the material, fountain, holy, though welling up from the foul earth — my Fuensanta! Good or evil though you be, I love you for mine, and you shall be mine!

Fuen.— Señor de Medina, it seems to me that my doubts increase; and, finally, my dignity impels me to put an end to this interview.

Gab.— Just as you say; I have already told you what I wished to say. Ah, no; there is something else! (*As if suddenly recalling something.*) Yes, this: That I wished to say good by, because I embark this very day at Barcelona for America.

Fuen.— You are going away? (*With vexation and pain.*)

Gab.— Don't be worried; I'll come back.

Fuen. (*trying to smile*).— You may be a great man, but you are very presumptuous. Who told you that I'd worry if you were gone?

Gab.— You; you yourself; your voice is trembling, your smile is forced; you want to feign indifference, disdain, but you cannot. Don't worry. The inability to lie is another perfection of my Fuensanta.

Fuen.— That's enough — enough.

Gab.— Just as you say. And now I must say good by. (*Taking her hand.*)

Fuen.— And why are you going?

Gab.— For your sake.

Fuen.— For my sake!

Gab.— To calm you; to develop all your confidence in my affection; to dissipate your doubts.

Fuen.— Thank you kindly; but I don't understand.

Gab.— Oh, they are little things — trifles — the prose of life. You are rich, I am not; I am going to make my fortune; and when I come back a man of means, you will have no reason to torture your soul with cavillations unworthy of you and of me.

Fuen.— But you?

Gab.— Yes; I shall come back immensely rich. I am going to exploit some mines in California; in two or three years at most — a millionaire. Oh, this is the easiest thing in the world for a man like me.

Fuen.— So you are an omnipotent being? (*Mockingly.*)

Gab.— Almost, almost. I say almost for the sake of modesty, so as to have that perfection in addition.

Fuen.— A perfect being! (*Laughing.*)

Gab.— How can I help that? Why deny it, if I am?

Fuen.— If you are so perfect, how could you fall in love with so imperfect a being as I?

Gab.— For that very reason. Because I am more perfect than you.

Fuen.— Ah! (*She does not know whether to laugh or be vexed. Finally she bursts out laughing.*)

Gab.— Don't laugh; it is the truth. For a being more perfect, more powerful, more exalted than oneself, one feels respect, admiration, devotion, filial affection; but not love, deep, divine. Those beings who are in some respects inferior to us, our infants, our children, these we love without limit; to the point of sacrifice, crime, death, annihilation. Why, do you believe that the God-man would have sacrificed Himself for another God, supposing that another God such as He could have existed? No; for man, imperfect, weak, full of misery, corrupted by sin, threatened with damnation; for man, yes; for man a God would die on the cross; for another God, never!

Fuen.— Dear me, they are not likely to say that you are flattering me! An original proposal, surely!

Gab.— They, — they — When we have more time I'll tell you what they are.

Fuen.— Miserable creatures. Aren't they?

Gab.— Provisionally you may suppose that they are. And now that I have taken leave of you, I must take leave of them. (*Approaches a bell and rings it; a servant appears.*) Tell them all — the ladies and gentlemen— to come in, that I must say good by. (*Exit servant.*)

Fuen.— I don't altogether understand you.

Gab.— You are right; it is very hard, I do not yet altogether understand myself.

Fuen.— Really?

Gab.— Really. What am I? Who am I? Here is a secret. (*Pressing his forehead.*)

Fuen.— Are you talking in earnest?

Gab.— Yes. I am — a problem.

Fuen.— By the time you come back you will have solved it. (*With a certain tenderness.*)

Gab.— Assuredly.

Fuen.— And you will tell me your secret?

Gab.— I swear it!

Fuen.— When?

Gab.— On our wedding-day.

Fuen.— Again. (*Laughing.*)

Last Scene

FUENSANTA, GABRIEL; *the rest entering*

Gab.— Ladies — gentlemen — I bid you good by. I leave this woman in your keeping. I know you well enough to divine that during my absence you will torment her without rest, without scruple, without pity. (*Movement of indignation and murmurs of protest among them all.*) No matter; it is a test to which Fuensanta must submit. Good by; I shall come back to make her mine. (*To all.*) Surround her; tighten up the thumbscrews. Good by, Fuensanta, my love; suffer and hope. (*Crosses through the midst of them all, turns, looks at* FUENSANTA, *and passes out, amid movements and protests of indignation and threats.*)

ACT II

(SCENE: *a palace of* FUENSANTA'S *in* BARCELONA *overlooking the harbor; the principal salon of the towers of the palace, in the form of a gallery enclosed by plate-glass, from which one sees the sea, the sky, and a wide horizon; in the background, a re-entering angle; on the left, the principal door, a large one; the right all glass, affording a view of the sea. In the front wings, right and left, doors leading to* FUENSANTA'S *apartments, to a billiard room, and to other salons. Luxurious furniture and ornaments.* TIME: *late afternoon.*)

SCENE I

DON MODESTO, ANGELES, *and a servant*

Servant.— The Señora is in her apartments; I will go tell her.

Mod.— No, there's no need of troubling her; we'll wait, as usual, till she comes out. (*Servant bows and retires.*)

Ang.— It's two days since I've seen Fuensanta. Why haven't you brought me? Was she worse?

Mod.— No, daughter, no. She is all right; that is, you know she's not all right — whims and fancies — of a woman who is beautiful, rich, and beloved of us all — for we couldn't do more for her, could we, sweetheart?

Ang.— Yes, I believe we could do more.

Mod.— Why, what could we do?

Ang.— Leave her in peace.

Mod.— You think that we annoy her? Are there any more affectionate kinsfolk in the world?

Ang.— I don't know — I don't know; it seems to me there are.

Mod.— Why, don't we try to divine her wishes? She forsook her elegant villa and came to this palace in Barcelona; thereupon to Barcelona all of us. She grew tired of the principal apartments and came up to this tower; we followed to the tower; she comes to this room, seats herself at this gallery to look at the sea; we surround her. Dine, she never dines alone; breakfast, one of us always accompanies her. We divide up the day and the night among us, and two or three kinsfolk are never out of this palace or this tower.

Ang.— But this is horrible, papa! It's the siege of a beleaguered fort, as Don Leandro says.

Mod.—Ah! Is that what he calls it? The siege! So he calls it a siege.

Ang.— I don't know what Don Leandro means, exactly; but I can guess. Besieging is worrying people, isn't it, papa? Now look, papa, the way you are worrying Fuensanta is enough to drive her mad. Ugh! Such solicitude makes you sick. I'd show you all — that is, not you, papa — but all the rest of them I'd show the door. (*Making the motion.*) And although she is the loveliest character, that's what she'll do at last — show us all —— (*As before.*)

Mod.— If we should leave her alone, she'd die of grief.

Ang.— Why, what more does she want than to be left alone, with her thoughts, with her memories, with her love letters? (*With a certain malice.*)

Mod.— Eh? With her love letters?

Ang.— Yes—with the letters — from him — from that man—from the other one — the one over there. But you do think I don't know anything? Or that I'm an idiot?

Mod.— You know more than you ought to know ——

Ang.— Oh, it's a sight to see! — she seated in the middle of this salon as if asleep, but she's not asleep; and all her dear relations sitting around with their eyes glued on the poor dear. Don Baltasar — ill-tempered beast! — glaring at her with his big tiger eyes, which shoot out a red gleam at the least contradiction; Don Esteban, as yellow as a pumpkin, with his affected smile, staring at her with his little straw-colored eyes; Doña Andrea, who always pretends to be very sad, and tells everybody that her dear Fuensanta is dying, looking at her with her eyes full of crocodile tears— she's getting old, you know, and has weak eyes; that idiot of a Paco, sighing and sighing, staring vacantly with eyes as white as a plaster cast's. And she, paying no attention to the red eyes, nor the yellow, nor the weak, nor the white, turning her blue eyes toward the ocean, to see whether the man with the eyes of flame has come into port. Are we going to see Fuensanta?

Mod.— Go by yourself. I dare not. You are giving us all such a black eye!

Ang.— Naturally enough. No — hush — I beg pardon — I'm going in there — and if she's in a good humor, I'll call you, shan't I? Good by. (*Exit, right, first wing.*)

Scene II

Don Modesto, *afterwards a servant*

Mod.— Dear me! These girls of the new generation go to school to the devil! The devil always was a great schoolmaster, and he never will lack pupils. I wonder who are on guard now? For it's the truth that we do take regular turns in mounting guard. (*Rings a bell.*)

Serv.— Did you call, Senor?

Mod.— Yes. Who are in there? Some one must have come.

Serv.— Yes, Señor, Doña Andrea and her son. They always happen in at this time and stay till dinner-time.

Mod.— Inclusive.

Serv.— Yes, Señor.

Mod.— Well, tell them I'm here, to see whether they are coming out, or whether they want me to come in.

Serv.— All right, Senor. They are in the library, looking at pictures.

Mod.— Very well. (*Exit* servant, *right, second wing.*) I'd rather meet them than Don Baltasar; he's a tiger. Ah! Here she comes now.

Scene III

Don Modesto, Doña Andrea, *and* Paco. — *The* servant *crosses; exit left*

And.— How do you do, Don Modesto? (Paco *gives him his hand without saying a word, and goes to the rear to take his seat in front of the plateglass.*)

Mod.— Señora — Paquito ——

And.— There's news. (*Mysteriously.*) The crisis is approaching, they tell me.

Mod.— Indeed!

And.— Our man is coming back — When? I don't know. But our man is coming back.

Mod.— Man — man?

And.— Poor child! (*Pointing toward* Fuensanta's *room.*) Among them all they are going to kill her. She could be so happy — my poor Fuensanta! And that dear son of mine could be so happy. (*Pointing.*)

Mod.— Is he unfortunate, too?

And.— His passion is consuming him; he neither eats nor sleeps.

Mod.— Why, he looks to me as if he's asleep right now.

And.— Listen; a creature like Fuensanta, nervous, idealistic, dreamy, what would she need?

Mod.— A dreamy husband!

And.— That dolt, that fool ——

Mod.— Señor de Medina?

And.— Exactly. Señor de Medina will be the finish of Fuensanta. He'll kill her before our eyes.

Mod.— Before he marries her? (*Pauses.*)

And.— No, afterward.
Mod.— What a misfortune that would be!
Paco.— Mamma, I'm going downstairs.
And.— Why?
Paco.— Because it's unbearable here. There's such a glare — and it's awfully hot.
And.— But you won't see Fuensanta?
Paco.— I'll see her at dinner-time. We are going to dine with her, aren't we?
And.— Of course.
Paco.— All right, then; good by.
And.— It pains you to see her disdainful, my poor boy!
Paco.— Yes,— it pains me; and I'd rather see her at the table — because she doesn't treat me badly at the table.
And.— Shan't I give her a message from you?
Paco.— Yes, tell her — something sad — something tender — something new. 'The fading of the day is like the falling of the leaves, and leaves are like illusions.' She'll understand. Good by; Don Modesto, won't you go with me? We'll have a nice little caviare — he prepares it finely — and it's a splendid appetizer.
Mod.— Thank you, a thousand times; I must talk with your mother.
Paco.— Very well, just as you like. I don't like this glare. I don't like this room, either. I prefer the dining-room.

Scene IV

Doña Andrea, Don Modesto

And.— The poor fellow is reduced to despair, deep despair. He puts on a brave face,— he controls himself.
Mod.— He controls himself very well.
And.— Ah, he is a fine character! Fuensanta doesn't realize Paco's worth. None of these people understand him, either. We are warring to the death. For I maintain that it would be an act of justice and morality to see that Fuensanta's money, which came from our family, shall return to our family; doesn't it seem so to you? Don't you feel that way?
Mod.— Yes, Señora, yes. Really, I believe I feel so.
And.— Don Modesto, the avarice of certain people grieves and repels one. When Fuensanta had that heart trouble, two months ago, Don Baltasar and Don Esteban were sure she was going to die; and they had determined to compel her to make her will. What cruelty! And besides, altogether useless!

Mod.— For you, yes; because you would be the heir, as the next of kin to the deceased husband. For them — for them — I'm going to put things from their point of view — it would not be useless. Lacking in charity and affection, to be sure — to be sure — but far from useless, it would be a most advantageous precaution.

Scene V

The same, a servant, Don Baltasar, Don Esteban

Serv.— Don Baltasar — Don Esteban. (*Announces them and retires when they enter.*)

Est.— Good day.

Balt. (*ill-humoredly*).— Good afternoon.

And.— O my good friends! (*Gives them her hand.*)

Mod.— You are a little late.

Est.— The usual hour.

Balt.— And Fuensanta?

And.— In her room with Angeles.

Balt.— The same old story; she's running away from us. The ingratitude of humanity! This struggle is wearing me out.

And.— Why, she's very kind to me.

Balt.— Señora — you are working for yourself and your son.

And.— I — I don't understand.

Balt.— I am a straightforward soul, as straight as the blade of a sword. I am a disinterested man; considerations of — of interest I abhor.

Est.— Perfectly straightforward and disinterested, believe it, Don Modesto?

Balt.— Don't you believe it, Don Modesto?

Mod.— Why not? Who doubts it? Believe it, Doña Andrea!

Balt.— Very well; I grant my protection to Fuensanta, because she is a poor woman, forsaken, weak, credulous, sick, almost at the point of death, and because she is my niece; that is to say, we are of the same blood.

Mod.— So are we.

Est.— We are one family, then, and that involves obligations.

Balt.— We opposed — I opposed her marriage to Gabriel because it would be an imprudence, madness, almost infamy. And in view of all this, I am turning myself into a knight-errant.

Est.— A knight-what?

Balt.— Knight-errant.

Est.— Ah! To be sure. Go on.

Balt.— And moreover, Doña Andrea, I declare it here solemnly, vehemently, definitively (*with continually increasing energy*), that just as I have opposed Fuensanta's marriage with Señor de Medina, I shall oppose Fuensanta's marriage with your son. I have said.

And.— Why?

Balt.— Because it would be madness.

And.— And also a disgrace!

Balt.— If you don't press me — I'll not go so far as to say that.

And.— And you would do well not to — even if I, I should press you.

Balt.— Why?

And.— Because I would not tolerate it.

Balt. (*mockingly*).— And Paquito would!

And.— Don Baltasar!

Balt.— Doña Andrea!

Est.— Keep cool, ladies and gentlemen!

Mod.— That's what I say, keep cool. Really there's no reason ——

Est.— Civil war! Most grievous conflict! All animated by the same noble desire; all watching over this infant; and, notwithstanding, carried away by excess of zeal, we are divided among ourselves; we are attacking one another. Worse still, we doubt one another! Can any one doubt the knightliness of Don Baltasar? (*All protest vehemently that they do not doubt.*) Can any one doubt the pure motives of Doña Andrea? (*As before.*) Does any one doubt the gentle, disinterested, and modest character of Don Modesto? (*The same protests of confidence.*) And of me, who has any doubts?

Mod.— Nobody!

And.— Good gracious, Don Esteban! Nobody!

Balt.— Very well, then, nobody. (*Ill-naturedly.*)

Est.— Then let us close our ranks, because the danger is greater than you imagine.

And.— Indeed? I suspected something.

Balt.— How?

Mod.— Let's have it!

Est.— I know that Gabriel is coming back; he has set sail in his yacht; and I don't know how it is he isn't here already.

And.— He's coming back a rich man?

Est.— A Crœsus! He was never poor; but he's such a scatterbrain, he had squandered his fortune, abandoned his rich mines in California, forgotten his business. He took the money fever; he went away, he worked, he struggled — and, as he is a man of exceptional ability, in one year he made himself a millionaire. So he's coming back; and here you are disputing.

Balt.— Well, let him come when he will, Fuensanta's fortune shall not be his. That is to say, Fuensanta shall not be his; for I'm defending, not the fortune, but the happiness, of my niece.

And.— And do you believe that he is coming for Fuensanta? That this whim of his will last?

Mod.— Yes, Señora, yes. All this time the two have been in correspondence.

Balt.— I see; a love affair. Then the attack shall be made upon this love affair, even though at the point of the sword. I am not going to let myself be robbed of Fuensanta's affection.

And.— Nor we. I'm not going to let myself be robbed of my son's happiness.

Mod.— No one shall rob me of anything — money or affection. Hear! Hear!

Est.— Coolness, prudence, and union.

Mod.— Union above all.

Balt. (*giving his hand to* DOÑA ANDREA.)—Union for the time being.

And.— For the time being. But when the danger is past ——

Balt.— Every one to his tent.

And.— Sh! (*Looking toward the rear.*)

SCENE VI

DOÑA ANDREA, DON BALTASAR, DON ESTEBAN, DON MODESTO, *a servant,* DON LEANDRO

Serv.— Will you please wait while I go tell the Señora? (*Exit, right.*)

Lean.— Doña Andrea. Gentlemen. (*All greet him coldly.*)

Mod.— My dear Don Leandro! (*He is the only one who makes any show of affection.*)

Balt.— It will be hard for you to see Fuensanta. She is not well.

Lean.— I know it; the last few days I have come frequently, and they have always told me — by your orders — the same thing; so that I have not been able to see her.

Balt.—- Of course.

Lean.— To-day, however, I am inspired by the hope that my visit will not be in vain. To-day, I believe, she will receive me.

Balt.— I doubt it.

Serv. (to DON LEANDRO).— She says that if you'll be so good as to wait, she'll come at once. (*Exit left.*)

Lean. (to DON BALTASAR).— You see? There are such things as presentiments. Mine, however, are not quite that; I had written, and she had answered that she would look for me.

Balt.— Then you had an engagement before you came. (DON LEANDRO *sits down.*) Oh, Fuensanta is perfectly at liberty to receive her friends. We haven't sequestered her. Do you understand?

Lean.— I suppose so.

Balt.— And as we too have something to talk about, and don't want to trouble you, we shall withdraw. Shan't we!

Est.— Immediately.

And.— Yes; let's go.

Mod.— We'll leave you in peace. (*To* DON LEANDRO.)

Lean.— Just as you like. (*They bow and retire, right, second wing.*)

And. (to DON MODESTO).— He has something up his sleeve. The plot thickens. (*Exeunt both.*)

Balt. (to DON ESTEBAN).— We shall have to act with decision.

Est.— With decision, but with prudence. (*Exeunt both.*)

Lean.— They'll not go very far. Poor Fuensanta! (*Closes the doors through which they have passed.*)

SCENE VII

DON LEANDRO *and* FUENSANTA

Fuen.— At last, and alone! How delightful! (*Looking around.*) Why did you have to ask to come to see me?

Lean.— I have come four or five times, and they've always told me that you were not seeing any one.

Fuen.— You! You, any time! It's they — they — who don't want me to see anybody, to talk with anybody! It's unbearable — believe me!

Lean.— Because you are very weak; too kind, I mean.

Fuen.— How can I help it? After all, they are my kinsmen. I am rich, they are not; it is very hard to turn them out of my house. I have not the courage to offend or humiliate anybody.

Lean.— But you are suffering.

Fuen.— I am suffering — but I should suffer even if they did not come. And who knows? Perhaps very soon I shall suffer no longer. (*Anxiously passionately, in a low tone.*) He is coming — Gabriel is coming; perhaps to-morrow, perhaps to-day. Perhaps before nightfall we shall see a yacht enter the harbor; it will be his. Just a little while ago I saw on the high sea a black point which grew bigger and bigger; and above the black point I fancied I could see a cloud of smoke; what joy I felt! How beautiful is the sea when our hope comes over its waves; an expanse of foam-capped blue, upon it a ship ploughing through the waves, in the ship a man who with confident heart is looking toward the port; within this man a heart that throbs in time to the strokes of the propeller, as if to say, ' Faster! Faster! They are waiting for me!'

Lean.— You are right, Fuensanta; according to my information it is quite possible that this yacht is his. He is keeping his word, and you doubted!

Fuen.— I doubted — but I doubt no longer; Gabriel is the man that I had dreamed. With you I have no secrets; you are a good friend, my only friend; and on this occasion you have acted toward me as a father. Thanks to you I know them — and I know Gabriel.

Lean.— Thank God!

Fuen.— But why did he go away? Why is he delaying his return so long? A year and a half; nearly two years! A lifetime, almost!

Lean.— Very short, at any rate.

Fuen.— Suffering lengthens the hours and turns them into centuries. When I was so ill, what anxiety, what despair! ' If I die without seeing him, without telling him that I love him!' That is—to say it to him—I have told him so many times — but in writing; and that does not satisfy. You put ' I love you ' in a letter, and you have to write one character, and then another, and it never conveys. ' I love you,' the lips say, and the soul goes out with it at once.

Lean.— That's the way I like to hear you talk!

Fuen.— O Don Leandro, what a shame! What am I saying! But it's because I have such confidence in you that when I talk to you it seems as if I'm talking to myself.

Lean.— You are perfectly right to love him with all your soul. This — this is the way of happiness.

Fuen.— Yes. I have come to love him with infinite passion. What you have told me about Gabriel, his absence, and his letters; his firmness and his energy; his strange, sublime thoughts — from all this it has come about that Gabriel is everything to me! Everything! Everything. I — I am not myself; my soul is merged in this man; if he fails me, it means that I am merged in nothingness, and therein shall I be overwhelmed forever, forever!

Lean.— If he could hear you — what happiness for him!
Fuen. (*pensively*).— Who knows!
Lean.— Again those ill-omened doubts!
Fuen.— Not at all. You don't understand. I'll explain myself. (*She turns toward the rear, then toward the right, and makes sure that the door is locked.*) Nobody hears us, nobody sees us. (*Twilight has fallen; it is almost night; the room is in shadow; through the glass of the background, the sea; vague light, some clouds.*) Almost darkness; I am glad of that; for darkness suits what I want to say. That's the way I pass my nights — doubting in the dark! Don Leandro, I love Gabriel as I have told you; no, as I have not told you and cannot express; there are no words, no accents to express it; the language of the lips is not that of the heart. In a word, I love him with all my heart. But does he love me the same as I love him? When I read some of his letters, it seems to me that he does; that it is a simple, human affection that goes from heart to heart, in which I get the better bargain, because I am not an exceptional, sublime being like Gabriel. When he descends to me in his letters, when he tells me of his life, full of exertion; of his excursions, of his remembering when he saw a flower like the one I wanted to pull that day, and of his tearing his wrists with pincers because he thought he had hurt me; of his kissing my portrait, my letters — commonplace things, you see: well, these things make me cry, and then I believe that he loves me really, and that we are going to be very happy. And then I throw my arms about his neck, and my heart presses his! Our hearts beat in unison! We are equal! He, Gabriel, I, Fuensanta! lovers to-day, husband and wife to-morrow! to live united, to die the same day!
Lean.— Why, I don't see what more you can say!
Fuen.— Yes, but other letters I don't understand. He says admirable things, stupendous things; they must be stupendous; but he speaks very little of me. It seems as if he is protecting me, that he is saving me; not that he loves me! Now I don't twine my arms about his neck, because he towers, towers above me; and I end by embracing his feet, humble, prostrate, and as if in adoration. His heart, if he really has a heart, has soared very high, and I can no longer reach it: The man has become a giant; he is not mine; he has risen to heaven. What matters it to me if his heart does soar to heaven if it be not against my own? Away up there, of what use is it to me?
Lean.— Look here; you are beginning to rave!
Fuen.— I believe you! So you may laugh at me, now that I have made a general confession.
Lean.— Was it a full confession?

Fuen.— I'll not tell you any more! You are not taking me seriously!

Lean.— Look; open your lovely eyes and look there.

Fuen. (approaching the background and looking).— Where?

Lean.— Over there — to the right. No, there's no doubt of it.

Fuen.— I don't see — I don't see anything. Don't deceive me! Don't joke, for heaven's sake, don't joke.

Lean.— Joke! No, Fuensanta! — But don't you see anything?

Fuen.— I don't know where you mean.

Lean.— To the right — a group of small craft.

Fuen.— Yes.

Lean.— Then a clear blue space — the trail of light where the moon is reflected.

Fuen.— Yes.

Lean.— Then two steamers almost together.

Fuen.— Yes — that's true.

Lean.— And a little farther a yacht, very well built.

Fuen.— Yes, I see it — a yacht! His yacht! Dear heaven, Gabriel's!

Lean.— No doubt; it must be his — the one you saw coming.

Fuen.— Yes,— yes,— the same! The stack is still smoking. Gabriel! Gabriel! At last! Dear Heaven, at last!

Lean.— Come, be calm; let us wait!

Fuen.— Wait! Wait! What are you saying? No! Enough of doubts! I want to know if it is he! Don Leandro, for heaven's sake — I beg of you — go down to the port! It is he! Make him come! Go!

Lean.— Yes, my child, I'm going; I'm going over there. (*Exit, rear, left.*)

Fuen.— Thank God! (*Looking through the plate glass.*) Yes — I am going to see him — to hear his voice! My dreams! My dreams now no longer dreams! What happiness, dear Lord! And they say there is no such thing as happiness! Anything makes us happy; the sight of a yacht that has come in; some puffs of smoke blown out of the chimney; a little trail of light on the water which seems to invite us to come thither — thither — to see Gabriel walking amid the stars! (*She stays close to the glass, gazing fixedly. All the glass, the sea, and the sky lighted by the moon; the front almost in darkness.*)

Scene VIII

FUENSANTA. *One by one, as indicated by the dialogue,* DOÑA ANDREA, DON MODESTO, DON BALTASAR, *and* DON ESTEBAN. *They come in silently and enter the shadow.* FUENSANTA *in the light, at the left*

And. (*approaching* FUENSANTA *gradually and speaking in a low tone; throughout the scene, except at the close, all speak in low tones.*) Fuensanta!

Fuen. (*half turning*).— Ah! it's you? (*Again turns to look toward the port.*)

And.— Did I startle you?

Fuen.— A little; you came in so quietly.

And.— Are you nervous?

Fuen.— Yes, a little.

And.— What are you looking at?

Fuen.— The sea and the sky.

And.— An exquisite night.

Fuen.— Exquisite.

And.— Shall I turn on the light?

Fuen.— No; the light from outside is enough for me.

And.— Not for me; and I'm afraid of the dark.

Fuen.— I'm not.

And.— What are you thinking about? (*All these questions in an affectionate, insinuating, low tone.*)

Fuen.— Nothing.

And.— Do you feel any pain?

Fuen.— On the contrary, joy.

And.— He is coming! (*Speaking even lower.*)

Fuen.— Yes.

And.— What madness!

Fuen.— Why so?

And.— Because he doesn't love you; scholars love nobody but themselves.

Fuen.— What do you know about it? (*Moving away from* DOÑA ANDREA *and going to the other side of the plate-glass, to the right.* DON ESTEBAN *has now entered, and is in the shadow, but near the glass wall.* FUENSANTA *at first does not see him.*) Ah! Why won't they stop!

Est.— Fuensanta!

Fuen.— There you are again! (*Turning.*) Oh, it's you!

Est.— Who did you think it was?

Fuen.— Andrea. (*Pauses.*)

Est.— Not a very bright night, is it?

Fuen.— Do you think so?

Est.— It seems to me there are a great many clouds.

Fuen.— But the moon is scattering them.

Est.— The sky will be covered after a while.

Fuen.— Who knows?
Est.— Shall we go in?
Fuen.— No.
Est.— Poor Fuensanta!
Fuen.— Poor! Why? You all say that I'm very rich.
Est.— Will you be vexed if I ask you a question?
Fuen.— I am rarely ever vexed.
Est.— Do you think of him all the time?
Fuen.— All the time.
Est.— My poor, dear child, you are going to be sadly disappointed.
Fuen.— Why? Why?
Est.— Because Gabriel doesn't love you. Men of genius, sublime men — have only one love — for their own genius, for their own glory. Other beings inspire them at best with compassion. Are you content with that?

Fuen.— That will do! (*Turns to the center and almost stumbles over* Don Modesto.)
Mod.— I beg pardon, my child!
Fuen.— Pardon me, Don Modesto. (*Sinks into an armchair.*)
Mod.— It's so dark I didn't see you. Shall I turn on the light?
Fuen.— I've already said no.
Mod.— Are you vexed with me?
Fuen.— With nobody.
Mod.— Are you in a bad humor?
Fuen.— Not in the least.
Mod.— You haven't had your letter? (*With gentle malice.*)
Fuen.— From whom?
Mod.— You know whom; when I saw you were in a bad humor I said to myself, ' I see; the other one hasn't written '— the man over there! My child, these men that know things don't know how to love; that's the only thing they don't know.

Fuen.— I've said twice already — that will do!
Mod. (*startled*).— I didn't know it; not to me — to Doña Andrea, maybe — to Don Esteban — to all these people walking around here like shadows. (*Rises and goes to the opposite side.*)

Balt. (*who has entered and exchanged some words with* Andrea *and* Esteban, *in a mysterious tone.*) You haven't imposed silence upon me, either. (*In a low tone.*)

Fuen.— Ah! You here too?
Balt.— I too; I too am walking about in the dark. As you don't care for light ——

Fuen.— No.

Balt.— Why not?

Fuen.— Because I don't. Because I am doing very well as I am; a whim, perhaps.

Balt.— Don't you care to see us? Our presence annoys you?

Fuen. (*moving away in disgust*).— I didn't say anything of the kind.

Balt.— But you thought it.

Fuen. (*growing more and more nervous*).— Every one has his thoughts.

Balt.— I can guess yours.

Fuen.— Perhaps so; since you are always speculating about what I am probably thinking!

Balt.— Because you think about some one you ought not to be thinking about.

Fuen.— About Gabriel.

Balt.— What misfortune, what ruin, what despair you are going to suffer!

Fuen. (*moving away from* BALTASAR; *she is on the point of breaking down.*)— Always the same!

Balt.— No, Gabriel cannot love, Fuensanta! No, do not create these illusions for yourself, poor child! For him you are an insignificant creature, an inferior being, a freak!

Fuen.— Ah! I can bear no more! my prudence has a limit; my patience is exhausted; my cup is running over! Stop! Stop! (*With increasing fury to the end of the scene.*) 'To make a martyr of this woman,' Gabriel said to you when he went away; and you are obeying his injunction marvelously! Well did he know you! Always possessed of the same idea, always the same intention! (*Turning about in the shadow. When she approaches any one, he steps back.*) At first Gabriel was a meddler, a hypocrite, an adventurer; he was trying to get my money, and nothing more. Avarice! Avarice! Ah! yes, avarice does exist in the world, but not in Gabriel! And now, when Gabriel is richer than I, when he cannot be accused of avarice and self-seeking, he is accused of being very learned and of being incapable of loving me, because scholars do not know how to love. And when it is proved that he loves, that he does love me, what new accusation, what new infamy? We shall see! we shall see! Come on with the new invention! Quick! Slander him, blacken his character, torment me! Quick! while the victim still has power of resistance! (*With extraordinary excitement.*)

And.— Fuensanta, what are you saying?

Mod.— For God's sake, for God's sake, don't be angry!

Est.— You judge us wrongly.

Balt.— You insult us, you are treating us shamefully; it is you who are slandering us.

Fuen.— I am insulting nobody! I am addressing nobody. I have no wish to slander anybody! I see nobody! This is why I wanted to be in the dark — so as to have courage to say to you what I have said, without knowing to whom I speak!

Balt.— You are speaking to us!

Fuen. (*with increasing excitement*).— I don't know who you are! I divine in the darkness shadows which trouble me; I hear voices which wound my ears, and my heart even more; I touch in the darkness garments which brush against me; and I need not say I am defending myself. And I fling my arms about, and I cry aloud, and I almost strike a face or a conscience! So much the worse for him who feels the blow! For whoever deserves the punishment I give him with the courage darkness lends me, him shall I likewise punish in the light of day, when I know him again by the mark of the blow! (*All speak, each clearly distinguishable:* 'Fuensanta!' ' Child!' ' For God's sake!' ' Fuensanta!') Silence! What I have said I said to whoever deserves it! (*All murmur:* 'She meant Baltasar!' ' She meant Andrea!' ' She meant him!' ' She meant me!' *almost at the same time.*)

And.— She meant Baltasar!

Est.— She meant it for Andrea!

Mod.— She means them!

Balt.— Me!

Fuen.— Silence! And I announce to you all that Gabriel is coming; that Don Leandro has gone to meet him; that in this room, alone with Angeles, I am going to receive him; that the day which Gabriel fixes shall be the wedding day; that I invite all my dear relations to my marriage to Don Gabriel de Medina! that till then, woe to him who shall utter a word, a single word against the man who is to be my husband! Therefore change your plans and respect him whom I respect and whom I love! And above all, don't trouble me, for the weakest beings may be the most terrible when brought to bay and reduced to despair! Ah, what people; my God, what people! (*Exit, right, weeping.*)

Scene IX

Doña Andrea, Don Baltasar, Don Esteban, *and* Don Modesto; *in the background, left,* Gabriel *and* Don Leandro, *who stop without being seen. All the rest have moved to the front*

Mod. (to Doña Andrea).— Fine things she said. She scared me.
And.— Don Baltasar didn't appear so fierce as usual.
Est.— That was a clawing talk! She has no paws, to be sure, but she drew out her claws! (*To* Don Baltasar.)
Balt.— It will be necessary to cut them.
Est.— Necessary, but dangerous. (Gabriel *asks* Don Leandro *a question in a low tone.* Don Leandro *shows him the electric light switch.* Gabriel *turns on the light; the stage is brilliantly illuminated. All turn in surprise.* Gabriel, *after turning on the light, breaks out into rather strident laughter.*)
Balt.— Who is that?
And.— Ah!
Mod.— It's he!
Est.— He!
Gab.— It is I. And I am He who turned darkness into light. (*Laughs again.*) 'Fiat lux, et lux facta fuit!' Let there be light, and there was light! I am come to the hearts and arms of my old-time friends as I ought to come, enveloped in splendor. I am that I am! (*His costume must be carefully worked out; it should be, not fantastic, but somewhat removed from the ordinary; it is a problem.*)
Lean.— Fuensanta is not here; I am glad of that.
And.— She went to her room a few minutes ago.
Lean. (to Gabriel).— Wait for me here. I am going to prepare her; she was very nervous; don't come in, yet; wait till I call you. I shall tell her that you are coming, but that you have not come yet.
Gab.— Just as you think best. (*Exit* Don Leandro, *right.*)

Scene X

Doña Andrea, Don Baltasar, Don Esteban, Don Modesto, *and* Gabriel. Gabriel *advances as if preoccupied, and sits down in the foreground. In his countenance, even in his costume, the premonitory symptoms of insanity are noticeable. The rest gaze fixedly at him*

Gab.— You are watching me with interest, with curiosity, even with fear, aren't you? (*Anticipating a movement of the others.*) No, it doesn't surprise me in the least. It is natural for you to look at me like that. I look at myself just that way when I find myself in front of a mirror. How peculiar, how inexplicable, that it should be I! For it to be some one else — it would be quite right. But that it should be I! Most curious! (*Laughs softly.*) Most curious!

And. (*to* DON BALTASAR).— What is he talking about?
Balt.— Indeed I don't understand him; I never understand this man.
Gab.— For if you knew who I am, how you would wonder! But I shall not tell you; it is my secret — a sublime, a formidable secret! Don't be alarmed, don't be alarmed, I am not going to tell you.
Est. (*to* DON MODESTO).— But what does he mean by all this?
Mod.— I don't know; I believe he is threatening us. To tell you the truth, I don't like it.
Balt.— And this secret?
Gab.— Hush! It is a secret. Let us speak of other things.
Est.— We have no interest in ferreting out your secrets.
Gab.— There is much to talk about. What an unexpected thing!
Balt.— What? What is unexpected? Go on! (*Impatiently.*)
Gab.— That I have come back. You did not count on my coming back. I always return; rather, I do not return, because I abide. To return is an imperfect way of abiding forever. Can one not stand still? Then he revolves. The whirlwind revolves, to return where it was; the wild beast circles about his prey until he leaps upon it. How much you must have circled about Fuensanta these two years! I have not; I have always, always been in possession of her soul, always within the chamber of her heart, giving impulse to its beats. For Gabriel, for Gabriel! Thus — thus — by day — by night — without ceasing — without ceasing —(*With his hand on his breast; drawing it away and bringing it back, as if imitating the pulsation.*) Evidently, if it had stopped beating she would have died.
Est. (*to* DON BALTASAR).— I believe he has come back worse than when he went away. Look at his face.
Gab.— You, in the meantime, are also standing firm in your place; you are who you are; I find you where I left you. Time leaves no trace upon you, Don Modesto, nor on you, Don Esteban; nor on you, Don Baltasar; nor on you, Señora — on you it is leaving its mark. Time is cruel!
Balt.— Señor de Medina, will you talk like other people, so that we may understand you? (*In an irritated tone.*)
Gab.— The same, the same as ever! The sanguinary, the violent, the impulsive! Selfishness and tiger-springs! This man is a force — a brute force, but still a force; he must be mastered with force.
Est.— Señor de Medina is a philosopher — and speaks as a philosopher — in figurative language — and, moreover, in general propositions, without reference to any one in particular.
Gab.— Also the same. The man who glides smoothly along — who tempers blood with bile; who, who coils himself up, and crushes when he is well coiled. For him, a fine, keen blade; his coils must be cut!

Balt.— My friend Don Esteban, if you call this philosophical language — and stand it, I must confess that you are more of a philosopher than Señor de Medina.

Est.— My dear Don Baltasar, seriously — I tell you, Gabriel is mad.

Balt.— That's an idea; that would be a solution. (Don Modesto *is withdrawing.*)

Gab.— Don't go, Don Modesto; for I'm not going to say anything to hurt or grieve you. You have a daughter who is an angel, and for the children's sake the parents can be saved, because the goodness of the children sprang from the parents. Perhaps it is because they gave it that they have none left for themselves — arid rocks which have dried up their vitals to feed fresh springs! Never fear, Don Modesto; petty creature, selfish, cowardly, avaricious — I forgive you for Angeles's sake!

Mod.— Thank you very much. My Angeles is worth a great deal! (*In terror. To* Don Esteban, *in a low tone.*) This man has gone mad.

Est.— A madman from the madhouse; they're happiest when they are giving trouble.

And.— My friend (*to Gabriel*) if we should all talk intelligibly — if we should all be reasonable ——— (*Gently.*)

Gab.— To be sure — to be sure. See how gently Doña Andrea speaks to me. Ah — and your son? The interesting Paco?

And.— Señor de Medina. (*In a pleading tone.*)

Gab.— No, don't be afraid; I shall say nothing about you or Paquito. You love your son dearly, indeed you do. It would be cruelty to mistreat Paquito; he is an innocent, inoffensive young man, who discourses with judgment and prudence. (*From the rear; in a mocking tone.*) Every sentence of his is an incontrovertible proposition! Paquito is Paquito! (*Moves to one side to* Don Baltasar *and* Don Esteban, *and speaks to them in a low tone.*) Paquito is an imbecile, a fool; she is cold, selfish, avaricious; he will be an idiot forever and ever; but she loves him as a mother, and the mother-love is sacred. God Himself would bow in reverence before the love of this mother for this son! They are two clods of earth, almost mud; but they are united by a circle of heaven! Silence! Don't say a word! (*In a low tone.*) Ah! Your son — Ah! Señora! — is my chosen friend. Call him for me — call him for me — for I wish to fold him to my heart!

And.— My friend! (*Gives him her hand; approaches the rest.*) You are become another man! How sensibly you speak!

Balt.— Señora, don't be an innocent! He was making fun of you!

Mod.— He told us that Paquito is a fool, and you — you, a woman without conscience!

And.— He? He said that?
Balt.— Yes, Señora.
And.— But this man is a rascal!
Balt.— A madman!
Est.— Madam! Yes!
Mod.— Look! (GABRIEL *keeps on walking and gesticulating.*)
And.— It's the truth.
Balt.— And we ——
Est.— We — nothing — quiet, non-committal — wait! He shall do everything — we, nothing!
Gab. (*stopping and looking at them*).— What are you plotting now?
Mod.— We — we plot!
And.— You believe we are a set of monsters — and you hate us, Señor de Medina!
Gab.— I hate! No, not I. Nor do I believe that you are such monsters; monsters don't exist. Yes, I shall know! You seem wicked, selfish, greedy. Granted you are all this; some would say that you are selfish ——
Balt.— Oh, yes, we have heard all that.
Gab.— But I deny it! I deny it before the world! Before the sea! Before the sky! Before God! Before myself! (*Becoming excited, and raving.*) You are not fundamentally wicked, you are — imperfect — or rather, incomplete!
Balt.— Not half bad!
Gab.— You understand!
And.— Not a word, Señor de Medina.
Gab.— Why, it's perfectly simple. If you break an exquisitely beautiful vase, will each piece be beautiful by itself? No; it will be shapeless, absurd, ridiculous! No, don't you deny that each piece will be ridiculous, because I am capable of making pieces of you, to convince you! (*Advancing toward them in fury. All recede.*)
Mod.— Certainly! Certainly! Ridiculous! (*Because* GABRIEL *is advancing upon him.*)
Gab.— Very well — and why? Because each piece is incomplete. It is the artistic vase, but incomplete. Eh! (*In a triumphant tone.*)
Est.— Certainly. Continue.
Gab.— If muddy pools are formed on the seashore in a depression of the ground, why are they muddy? Because they are so? No, because they are separated; because the crystals of water are broken; because each pool is an incomplete river! Join them; give them volume, give them a channel,

give them a current, and the river shall be blue and sparkling, the joy of the valley, the refreshment of its banks, the mirror of the sky!
And.— So we are this blue, sparkling river?
Gab.— No, you are still, like the pools.
Est.— What a pity. (*With a certain mockery.*)
Gab.— But don't be grieved; I will open a channel for you. Only you must be perfectly passive, you must not interrupt me in my work; because if the channel stops half made, if it turns out very shallow, it will be a ditch rather than a river-bed. (*In a deep, threatening tone. All recede.*)
Balt.— You say nothing but nonsense ——
Est.— But philosophic nonsense, which gives you the appearance of a scholar. We don't care for it.
Balt.— You are right. (*In a loud voice.*) Señor de Medina, things have come to the point at which you must speak with perfect clearness!
Gab.— Clearness! But you have darkened your understanding and blackened your consciences! Clearness — Fuensanta, who is all light; clearness, I, because I am I.
Balt.— Señor de Medina, we resolutely oppose your marriage with Fuensanta. (*Wishing to provoke him.*)
Gab.— Naturally enough. And why?
Balt.— We have no faith in the loyalty of your conduct.
Gab.— That is plain. You need not believe in me.
Balt.— We consider your love a pretence.
Gab.— A pretence?
Balt.— A fraud!
Mod.— Just so! A fraud! (*Seeing* GABRIEL *fix his eyes upon him.*) So Don Baltasar says!
Balt.— You feel no love for Fuensanta!
Est.— Or for anybody. You don't know how to love.
Gab. (*aroused*).— I don't love Fuensanta! Why, I am all love! My soul is dissolved in tenderness! What more? Why I am capable of feeling genuine affection even for you, of taking you in my arms and pressing you till you choke; even of merging you in myself! (*With the violence of madness.*) But you, why do you believe that God is so great? He is great, He is ineffable, He is infinite, because of His love; because it is He who loves the most; because it is He who suffers the most for His love; because when He saw that the void was not mere nothingness, He wept upon it and fructified it. Ah, miserable creatures! To deny that I can love, that I know how to love, is to open the floodgates of my wrath! Woe to you if you loose it! You shall be little bits, you shall be mud, you shall be

cinders, you shall be ashes! Nothing! nothing! What you were — what you are going to be again!

Est.— Here comes Fuensanta!

Gab.— She! She! Fuensanta! Fuensanta! Ah! What dew in my soul!

Last Scene

The same, Don Leandro, Fuensanta

Lean.— Here she is!

Fuen.— Gabriel!

Gab.— Fuensanta! (*They rush together and embrace. The rest watch them anxiously.*)

Fuen.— At last!

Gab.— At last! I have kept my word!

Fuen.— And I shall keep mine.

Gab.— Do you believe in me?

Fuen.— Yes, I do.

Gab.— They won't believe in my love for you. (*Gently. The sight of* Fuensanta *has calmed him.*)

Fuen.— What difference does that make!

Gab.— Don't worry yourself over them.

Balt.— We don't believe; no. (*All say no.*)

Fuen.— I said before that I would not suffer it ——

Gab.— Be calm, be calm, my darling; anger makes your eyes blaze; I like them gentle.

Est.— This man doesn't get angry.

Fuen.— You are right — just as you like. But you don't know how I have suffered!

Gab.— Your suffering is over now. (*Turning to all the rest.*) This woman is to be my wife.

Est.— No!

Balt.— No! (*The rest say no.*)

Fuen.— Ah! Gabriel, don't look at them!

Gab.— Don't worry over them. (*With great repose and superiority.*) Fuensanta shall be my wife. But I do not wish to dominate or fascinate her, as you suppose. She shall be mine through the drawing of our love, by her own volition. And to remove all doubt I shall leave the house at once.

Fuen.— No!

Gab.— I must. I wish you to be perfectly free. I am going back from here to my yacht, and I shall stay in it until the wedding day.
Fuen.— No, Gabriel! (*Passionately.*)
Gab.— I tell you, yes.
Fuen.— Just as you wish. You are to command.
Gab.— And I shall come back within a few days.
Fuen.— Never to leave me again.
Gab.— Never! And until then, farewell, my Fuensanta!
Fuen.— Farewell!
Gab.— Ah! (*Turning to the rest.*) But not alone; no, indeed. You shall go with me, to return with me the day of the wedding.
Balt.— We —— (*Protesting.*)
Fuen.— You will obey him who is to be my husband.
Gab.— Now you have your orders. Straight in front of me! Look, Fuensanta, how I am driving your tormentors! The flock of wretches; I, the shepherd of the black flock, driving them before me. Don't shy! I shall be lashing your shoulders — Shoulders, no — the loins for beasts. Out! Out! Farewell, Fuensanta!
Fuen.— Farewell!
Gab.— Farewell!

ACT III

(SCENE: *the principal salons of* FUENSANTA'S *palace. Three doors in the background, through which one sees into another salon; behind that, and separated from it by a row of pillars, a third salon. Brilliant illumination, luxurious furnishings, articles of virtu. The first salon in the foreground is a small salon or cabinet with side doors, which lead to* FUENSANTA'S *apartments.*

TIME: *the night of the wedding. If it is desirable to shorten the interval between acts, the decoration of the previous act may be retained.*)

SCENE I

DON LEANDRO, a lackey *in formal black livery*

Lean.— Has Señor Don Esteban arrived?
Serv.— Yes, Señor.
Lean.— Very well; ask him for me to be so good as to come at once; I am waiting for him impatiently.
Serv.— Yes, Señor. (*Exit, rear.*)
Lean.— I must anticipate the infamous proceedings of these people. I shall speak to him decisively. I have no confidence in any of them, and less in Don Esteban than in any of the others.

Scene II

Don Leandro, Fuensanta, *who enters, very much agitated, on the right. My impression is, that she should not be dressed in white, because she is a widow; but I turn this problem over to the actress*

Fuen.— Have you had your talk with Don Baltasar yet?

Lean.— Not with Don Baltasar, no; but I have called Don Esteban. Of all your relatives, beware most of him.

Fuen.— We ought not to invite any of them. After what they have done, they are nothing more to me.

Lean.— Avarice blinds and dominates them.

Fuen.— Why, it sets your brain in a whirl! To think that they would have dared — what they have dared! You know it; they have secured an attorney, and have lodged a complaint: 'That Gabriel is mad, and that the marriage is impossible;' and they have almost subjected Gabriel to an expert examination. What a humiliation!

Lean.— If they should hear you, the marriage would not be solemnized; and that on the ground of madness — not Gabriel's, but yours.

Fuen.— But tell me, Don Leandro, what are they doing right now?

Lean.— What are they doing? What do you know about it?

Fuen.— I know everything; because poor Angeles has told me everything she has heard from her father; I questioned Andrea, and she confessed the plan.

Lean.— But what is it?

Fuen.— That these people have arranged for an alienist to come in with the guests — even, I believe, with the judge's sanction — to observe — a notary to make affidavit of what happens. But what are they thinking about? Is there any law for this?

Lean.— Come, don't be so excited.

Fuen.— I am going to drive these two persons out of my house, and my relatives with them.

Lean.— Don't make a scene! That is what they would like!

Fuen.— No matter! I'll not put up with it!

Lean.— That is to say, Gabriel will find out about it; he is not mad, but when the occasion demands, has the spirit of all the devils, grows excited, becomes violent.

Fuen.— To be sure. You are right! No, my God, no! I will have patience — patience — patience!

Lean.— It is only two or three hours. You will be married, you will take the train, and then to Paris, to London.

Fuen.— Yes, yes; that is the best.

Lean.— Besides, I have called Don Esteban and I shall try to find some good way to get rid of these two individuals.

Fuen.— Exactly. How good you are!

Lean.— Listen; what you must do is to look Gabriel up, and tell him something of what is going on.

Fuen.— He knows all!

Lean.— So much the better. Well, then, advise him to leave off for to-night his philosophizing, his sublimities — to descend to earth and talk like every one else.

Fuen.— That's it exactly. I shall convince him that at least for to-night he must make an effort to be foolish, commonplace.

Lean.— Enough if Gabriel is natural, simple, easy. Lord, such is life.

Fuen.— Very well; don't worry any more — natural, simple, prosaic— I shall tell him, and he will obey me. May it pass quickly, may this night pass quickly! (*Excitedly.*)

Lean.— Now go away; here comes Don Esteban, and I shall be able to speak to him more freely if you are not here.

Fuen.— Yes, Señor, yes. Good by. I'm not forgetting it, no. Natural, simple. Oh, well, like everybody else. (*Moving toward the right.*)

Lean.— Quick! Go, child, go!

Fuen.— Natural, simple, commonplace, my Gabriel! What a shame! what a shame! (*Exit.*)

Scene III

Don Leandro, Don Esteban

Est.— Did you wish to speak to me, my dear Don Leandro?

Lean.— Yes, Señor.

Est.— Well, then, here I am at your service.

Lean.— I shall be very brief and very frank, and I shall proceed at once to business.

Est.— That suits me perfectly, because we shall have very little time at our disposal. Before a half hour — the solemn ceremony. So let's see ——

Lean.— Don Esteban, you have done a wicked deed. And to-night you are bringing about a scandal.

Est.— But what are you talking about? Indeed, I don't know how to answer you, my good friend.

Lean.— You preferred through — a third person — a formal charge against Gabriel; that is to say, you made out that he was mad. Don Esteban, there is no excuse for that!

Est.— Let us speak frankly. This act, which I disavow,— is not mine. The real culprits are Doña Andrea and Don Baltasar.

Lean.— But it is certain that it has been done.

Est.— Perfectly certain; and it was not only an indignity, as you say, but a piece of stupidity. Who could suppose that in view of an expert examination, slight and utterly superficial, by two or three alienists, a man worth twenty millions is going to be declared mad? (*With a mocking smile.*) Don Leandro, a rich man, an immensely wealthy gentleman, is *ipso facto* honorable, learned, mentally sound.

Lean.— Be that as it may, the plot was abortive.

Est.— And deserved to be. A man like Gabriel could not be declared mad, even if he were so, except by surprising him in an unmistakable attack of madness.

Lean.— Don Esteban!

Est.— For example, only a short while ago Gabriel and Don Baltasar met face to face in one of the salons. They stopped and glared at each other; and how they did glare! What an expression on Don Baltasar's face! And what an expression on Gabriel's face to-night! Pale, almost livid, his eyes gleamed like a tiger's. I have always maintained that he is not mad; understand that; nevertheless, believe me, he had the countenance of a madman (*smiling*); that was what inspired fear. And I thought, if he should throw himself upon Don Baltasar, and strangle him — for instance — who could be convinced that he is not mad? So I shall try to set their minds at rest; could I do more, Don Leandro?

Lean.— In very truth you could do no more. (*Significantly.*)

Est.— After the danger was past I laughed heartily, thinking: 'Suppose Gabriel strangles Don Baltasar — what luck!'

Lean.— To be sure (*aside*). To be sure; the marriage impossible and one co-heir the less.

Est.— Well, there you have it.

Lean.— And in the event anything happens, you have brought a physician and a notary. One of the two would be enough, wouldn't he, if the case came to the test, to annul the marriage?

Est.— Didn't I show you the list? I said to you, perhaps, 'I wish to invite this man or that, as friend or kinsman?'

Lean.— No, Señor, that was Don Modesto.

Est.— Ah! Then ——

Lean.— Be that as it may, these two gentlemen must be withdrawn.

Est.— Good heavens, my friend, how is it possible? Are you going to make a scene? The wedding will take place in a few moments. Calm yourself, I beg of you. Look, some of the guests are coming to these salons. You are a man of the world and of commonsense. Advise Gabriel to be very prudent and nothing will happen. (*Giving him his hand.*) I presume that I have not lost your esteem.

Lean.— You have not lost it. (*Aside.*) Because you never had it.

Est.— Whereupon, keep perfectly cool.

Lean.— Yes, Señor, you are right; perfectly cool; and to-morrow we shall all have a talk.

Scene IV

The same. In the background, in the salons of the hindmost wing, ladies and gentlemen are gathering. On one side Don Baltasar *advances with* Doctor Torres; *on the other,* Gabriel, *with* Paco. *Among the ladies in the background are* Andrea, Fuensanta, *and* Angeles. Don Esteban *goes to meet* Don Baltasar *and* Doctor Torres. Don Leandro *joins* Gabriel *and* Paco; *but these three stay in the central salon*

Est.— My dear Torres, have you had any occasion to observe Señor de Medina? (*The three in the foreground.*)

Torres.— A little.

Balt.— Have you observed him sufficiently to form an opinion?

Torres.— Not sufficiently, no. But I have observed — I have observed — so far as I could.

Est.— And what? Come, the truth!

Torres.— My friends, the truth is, that my situation in this house is very difficult, not to say irregular. I don't know why I have come. I should have gone before now had not Don Baltasar detained me. I am sequestered! It is a fact that you have me sequestered.

Balt.— You are here officially — by judicial order — to prevent a crime, a veritable crime.

Torres.— No, that is not true; I am not here officially, I have told you; I have explained it to you three or four times. I am here out of friendship for you, out of complaisance — out of weakness, I should rather say.

Est. (*restraining* Don Baltasar, *who protests*).— But at any rate, what is your opinion? Gabriel is — isn't it a fact? (*Making signs to indicate mental disorder.*)

Torres.— It is a very delicate matter; an examination would be necessary before venturing an opinion — and I have seen him in passing, have heard him utter a few sentences, nothing more. What do you wish me to say? To formulate a definitive opinion? It is asking too much of me.

Balt.— You acknowledged to me a little while ago that Gabriel is mad; mad, just the way it sounds.

Torres.— Good heavens, Don Baltasar! I did not say that. Moreover, this case is certainly not what is commonly known as madness. People in general apply the term madman to violent persons, to those who are delirious; to those poor sick creatures who go about with their hair in disorder and standing out, with their lips drawn, foaming at the mouth, emitting unearthly shrieks of laughter, with their hands clenched, their bodies trembling — and Gabriel is certainly not one of these madmen.

Balt.— Evidently not; but you said that in your opinion it was — it was a form of madness; therefore it is madness.

Torres.— I said something of the kind. But one must observe — one must observe.

Est.— Very well, then, continue your observations; here he is, coming his way. (*The three retire, while* GABRIEL *and* LEANDRO *advance, leaving* PACO, *who joins a group of ladies.*)

Torres. (*apart to* DON ESTEBAN).— Gabriel is mad; and perhaps before the close of the evening — in a word, we shall see. It is a very peculiar case; but don't say anything to Don Baltasar, because he is hopelessly mad. (*Laughing.*)

Lean (*drawing* GABRIEL *toward him*).— Listen, listen, Gabriel; a word or two.

Gab.— What do you want? Why do you separate me from Paquito? He is very entertaining. This youth shall sit beside me throughout the ages, for my diversion and joy ——

Lean.— Come; be sensible, or I shall believe what these people assert.

Gab.— What do they assert?

Lean.— That you are mad.

Gab.— And why should I not be so? Do you know what madness is? Does Don Esteban? Does that doctor they have brought, who has been looking at me for some little while, his eyes bulging with stupid curiosity?

Gab.— Then take me to Paquito. (*With the stubbornness of an idiot.*)

Lean.— Again! You'll make me lose patience!

Gab.— That's what you — wanted, you and Fuensanta; you asked me to say nothing to-night but commonplaces, to call ugly women beautiful; fools, men of talent; everybody a friend, even though I don't know him; everybody agreeable, everybody my dear sir, my lord! Very well; I am reviewing my lesson with Paquito; who could be a better teacher! Come to me, model and prototype of insipidity!

Lean.— Gabriel! Gabriel!

Gab.— Ah! Never fear; don't be alarmed; I have to do such things to-night, to utter such commonplaces, so as to make myself agreeable to everybody. (*Turning.*) Paquito!

Lean. (*holding him back*).— Come, Gabriel! I understand your resentment, your state of excitement! It is a horror, a torment; but have patience, my son.

Gab.— Patience! Why? To what end? I shall be what I wish to be! Genius? Then a genius! Fool? Then a fool! What I please! My will is law! I am that I am! (FUENSANTA, *who has been anxiously watching the scene from the rear, approaches* GABRIEL *in anguish, when he raises his voice.*)

Lean.— Do you see? It is your saying these things that the others don't understand, which makes them suppose — what they suppose. That is why, when I passed Torres a little while ago, I heard him say something, I don't know what, about 'the monomania of greatness.'

Gab. (*laughing harshly*).— Ah! That's what he said, is it? Poor doctor! I am going to give San Cosme and San Damian a companion! When I have time, I am going to arrange the heavenly court beautifully!

Lean. (*looking at him*).— I don't understand you! Indeed, I don't understand you!

Fuen.— Gabriel!

Gab.— (*In a gentle tone*). Fuensanta! My Fuensanta!

Fuen.— For God's sake, Gabriel, don't raise your voice! Everybody's attention is centered in you; everybody is watching you; every one is interpreting in his own way.

Gab.— And what matters it! Curiosity is a great thing! You don't know what it is — how much curiosity is worth!

Fuen.— Yes, but it is a hostile curiosity, of evil intent! Do you know what they say — what they plotted! For God's sake, Gabriel, for God's sake, prudence! It is an unbearable torture; I know it. (*All anxiously, in a low tone*).

Gab.— Torture! Punishment! That is the supreme blessing, my Fuensanta! For my Fuensanta I should wish to suffer all torments! To endure all sorrows! My body on the cross! There, nailed, pouring out my life blood! And within my breast, against the heart, another little cross, with my heartstrings nailed to it! And here, here (*pressing his head*), for every idea its tiny cross! All of my being undergoing punishment for my Fuensanta! In every fiber a writhing of pain! To suffer unending tortures for the being we love, this is to love as God loved His creatures! Listen and, mark you, as I love you. (*In a low tone, vibrant, persuasive, terrible.*)

Fuen.— Yes, it is true, Gabriel; but lower, lower; don't let them hear you!

Lean. (*moving away, and looking at a group of gentlemen in the rear*).— This Gabriel — this Gabriel! It is frightful to hear him; one who did not know him would probably believe what they say is true. He seems mad — yes, he seems mad.

Gab.— Then don't be troubled, my darling; let them scoff at me; let them humiliate me, call me mad. Are you sure that I am not?

Fuen.— Hush — hush! Don't say that! Do you take pleasure, too, in tormenting me? Don't look at me like that! It pains me, it frightens me!

Gab.— My poor darling!

Lean. (*approaching with two ladies and with* ANGELES).— Then come and we will introduce you, and you shall talk with him.

First lady.— We shall be highly delighted. We have heard many very romantic stories about Señor de Medina. (*The three approach.*)

Fuen.— For God's sake, Gabriel! Señora de Almeida and the Baronesa are coming — be careful! You'll follow my advice?

Gab.— I shall. For you, all sacrifices.

Fuen.— Here they are now.

Lean.— My dear Gabriel, Señora de Almeida and the Baronesa del Romeral wish to make your acquaintance. (GABRIEL *bows.*) Señor de Medina —— (*Presenting him; all bow.*)

First lady (*apart to the second*).— Let's see what he says.

Second lady (*apart to the first*).— Yes; let's see what he says.

Gab.— Ladies, it is an honor for me to place myself at your feet. I have wished it for a long time. The fame of your discretion and your beauty — (*Bowing.*) Ah, yes — they whetted my desire!

First lady.— You are very good.

Second lady.— As good as discerning.

Gab.— My discernment, Señora, embraces the whole world in its range.

Fuen. (*in a low tone to* GABRIEL).— Very good — so — so!

First lady (*to the second*).— He is very polite — and they said he was mad!

Second lady (*to the first*).— Calumnies! Ah, society!

First lady.— We have already congratulated Fuensanta.

Second lady.— And after meeting you we congratulate her anew.

Gab.— But you should have congratulated me.

First lady.— Who doubts it!
Second lady.— These scholars seem absent-minded — but they know what they are about.
Fuen.— If you please, suppose we stop the congratulations just here.
Gab.— Ladies — such honor. (*Taking leave.*)
First lady.— Señor de Medina, such gratification.
Second lady.— I have had the greatest pleasure.
Gab. (*somewhat nervous*).— Ladies, the gratification and the pleasure and the honor — and everything that we have said — and all that we failed to say for lack of time — all mine, all mine! I leave you with the angels (*pointing to* ANGELES) and in heaven (*pointing to* FUENSANTA) I could not leave you in a better place or in better company. I am going to them — to the people who are looking at me — who are in search of me ——
Fuen.— Yes, those gentlemen are calling for you. (*A little worried*). The ladies will excuse you.
Gab.— Ladies — (*Withdrawing.*) Paquito — where is Paquito! I need a new source of inspiration. (*Exit.*)
First lady.— He is very agreeable.
Second lady.— Very agreeable.
Ang.— He hadn't really talked to you! He says such lovely things! He is not quite at his ease with you yet, but you shall see — you shall see!
Fuen. (*aside*).— How frightened I am! He was already beginning to grow restive. (*Exeunt the four ladies, laughing and talking.*)
Gab. (*who has caught* PAQUITO).— Come here! Come with me, my dear young fellow, genius of shallowness, muse of insipidity, model of vacuity, guardian of nothingness; inspire me, inspire me; I yearn for your sublime knowledge, that my speech may resound with hollowness and my thought take the guise of a harlequin's; come with me to the masquerade!
Paco. How jocular Señor de Medina is! (*A group of gentlemen, among whom is Don* LEANDRO, *block his passage.*) I'm not taking it very kindly. (*Aside.*)
First gentleman.— Señor de Medina ——
Gab.— Ah — my dear, dear friend! (*Giving him his hand.*)
Second gentleman.— I wish you much happiness.
Gab.— Ah, my dear, dear friend!
First gentle.— Scholars marry too!
Gab.— They have to be like the fools in something.
Second gentle.— Don't be skeptical!
Gab.— Since we live among men!
Lean. (*somewhat restless*).— Let us respect the sanctity of marriage; these jokes for to-morrow.

First gentle.— And if he marries to-morrow, to-morrow will be the day after. (*Laughing.*)

Gab.— A bad moment to recall Don Juan!

Lean.— Gabriel is right.

Gab.— Respect me, gentlemen, respect me. (*In jest but changing his tone.*) Don Leandro, try to induce them to respect me, for if not — Gentlemen, what less could I ask! I could ask everything — and I ask nothing more than respect.

Lean.— We have no respect for you here — so move on. (*In jest, but trying to draw him away.*)

Gab.— It will be better — because there are no friends yet! there are no friends!

Fuen. (*who has followed him with her eyes.*)— Gabriel ——

Gab.— Love is my salvation. (*Approaches* FUENSANTA.)

Second gentle.— Why, there's nothing wrong with him. (*To the others, referring to* GABRIEL.) He speaks naturally.

First gentle.— I agree with you; and he is a man of great talent.

Lean.— A great talent and a great heart.

First gentle.— So everything they've been saying ——

Lean.— Outrageous! Calumnies! (*Moves away.*)

Est. (*in the rear, to the physician*).— How does he impress you?

Torres.— This evening happens to be a lucid interval; it is an intermittent case.

Gab. (*to* FUENSANTA).— I was imbecility itself; and now they don't take me for a madman, my life!

Fuen.— I'm so glad! What a lesson for these miserable creatures! You must always be thus.

Gab.— Always! Renounce being what I am! You ask me for the impossible! No, don't say that, Fuensanta! It is a blasphemy!

Fuen.— For God's sake, hush! (*Looking at him with something of terror.*) I said it wrong — for to-night, only for to-night; for me, for me! Will you? (*All this in a low tone; she supplicating, worried, tearful, thoroughly frightened.*)

Gab.— Very well; for to-night, very well. (*Calming himself.*) What is a night to me, or a century! Do you want a century? Then a century! For me the centuries are everlasting! I put my hand into eternity, I turn it about — and centuries, centuries, centuries!

Fuen. (*looking at him in terror*).— Gabriel!

Ang. (*entering precipitately; speaks to* FUENSANTA *in a low tone.*) Yes— now it is — come — they are waiting for you ——

Fuen. (without taking her eyes from GABRIEL).— Yes — I'm coming at once — My God! What is the matter with Gabriel? The poor fellow has been acting a part and repressing himself all the evening; and he is quite exhausted! He is quite exhausted! That is all! Gabriel!

Gab. (absentmindedly).— What? FUENSANTA *says something in his ear.*) Ah! good! let's go!

Lean. (coming up).— The solemn moment has arrived! I — I will lead you to the altar! Take my arm!

Fuen.— Yes — you — come — (*The two go toward the rear;* FUENSANTA *turns several times to look at* GABRIEL; *this exit is left to the actress's judgment.*)

Gab.— Now they are taking Fuensanta away from me! Are they taking her away? And who will take me? (DON ESTEBAN, DOÑA ANDREA, DON MODESTO, *and* PAQUITO *approach and gather around* GABRIEL. DOCTOR TORRES *remains at some distance watching.*)

And.— You? We.

Est.— Your good friends.

Paco.— For this solemn moment, who like us?

Gab.— Who like me? Who like God?

Mod.— Faster, my friend ——

Gab.— Forward — (*speaking to himself*). 'And he entered with palms into Jerusalem!' Forward! What a court of honor. You — and you — and all! (*Again abstracted.*) Yes,— but 'he went out with the cross!' (*As if talking to himself.*) Here, come, come! (*Exeunt all, laughing, through the rear; whence the rest of the company have been retiring.*)

Balt.— Not I! And you? (*To* TORRES.)

Torres.— I, yes; yes, I am. It is very curious; very curious. What an extraordinary case! (*Exit, behind the rest.*)

SCENE V

DON BALTASAR; *a moment after,* PACO

Balt.— Not I! Not I! I'll not be present at this farce! There's no justice nor reverence nor common sense in it! And this is permitted? And this marriage is being solemnized? What disgrace, what an absurdity, what complications for the future! Why, do you have to talk with this unfortunate more than five minutes to realize that he is demented? He is very astute, immensely so! To-night he has feigned sanity admirably. But I'll not allow it. Away with the mask — and if not, a sword-thrust!

There's some meaning in the saying: ' The madman is sane where penalty is concerned.' If Torres does not suffice, if the judge will not hear reason, if there are no laws, if there is no decency, if there is nothing, I'll take charge of the case — I! Come, keep cool! It seems to me that it's about to give me congestion. (*Seats himself and takes his head between his hands.*)

Paco.— Hello, Señor Baltasar, are you not going to be present at the ceremony?

Balt.— No, Señor, I am not going to be present. And from here I protest.

Paco.— What help for it, Don Baltasar! Why, they are stronger than we; and force, I have always said — force is force.

Balt.— You are resigned?

Paco.— When there is no remedy, what remedy is there?

Balt.— That is to say, it is all right. You are always judicious.

Paco.— It is on this account that mamma says that I am like an old man: on account of the moderations of my passions. Gabriel has told me a thousand times, that I am very thoughtful.

Balt.— Why, if Señor de Medina has said so — Ah, then ——

Paco.— Children and fools speak the truth. Of course, children as children ——

Balt. (*impatiently*).— Yes, and the fools as fools. Oh, yes, I see now that you are very thoughtful.

Paco.— I don't enjoy turning things upside down — because when one turns things upside down — everything, everything gets turned upside down.

Balt.— Of course. And you are turning my patience upside down.

Paco.— Why, what would you have me do? You have suffered in your interests — I have suffered in my interests and in the affections of my heart. And when one suffers in the affections of his heart — his heart is much affected.

Balt.— Now I understand; but you have had your consolation. Fuensanta has given you, for it was a gift, two hundred thousand dollars. This is a great aid to your spirit of resignation.

Paco.— What other object has resignation but that of resigning oneself?

Balt.— And now you are making love to the Baronesa de Romeral, the rich widow.

Paco.— She is a charming creature. How attentively she listens to me! It is no merit of mine, but she appears fascinated. She closes her eyes when I speak, so as not to lose a word. And not because I say things ——

Balt.— I should rather think so. And that's enough. You are telling me things I don't care a rap about, and all the time — in there — Damn it!

Paco.— Don't be annoyed, Don Baltasar.
Balt.— This boy is an idiot!

Scene VI

Don Baltasar, Paco, *and* Don Modesto

Balt.— Is the ceremony over?
Mod.— Not yet. That sort of thing moves me deeply. That's my nature.
Balt.— And Gabriel: how about him? What does he say? How is he behaving?
Mod.— Pretty well.
Balt.— He is saying no fantastic things?
Mod.— He says nothing; he looks, bows, smiles — Nothing; just like anybody else.
Balt.— These madmen are terrible! Their monomania gives them an air of dead seriousness, and they trick everybody. This is enough to make me lose my senses.
Mod.— Don't be worried, Don Baltasar.
Paco.— What will you gain by worrying? Nothing. Well, when one does not gain, one loses.
Balt.— So that you have not noted a single — alarming symptom in Gabriel?
Mod.— None. That is to say — that is to say ——
Balt.— What?
Mod.— He is very pale, almost livid; and his eyes gleam so. Many ladies are saying: 'How his eyes shine!' And some: 'It is from happiness!'
Balt.— From happiness! The human race is mad! And nothing more?
Mod.— Yes. When he entered the chapel, he went up to the altar, bowed above the cloth, leaned his forehead upon his hand, and remained in that position for a moment; in meditation, in adoration — I don't know what.
Balt.— Ah! And what did the people say then? I suppose it aroused some wonderment in them?
Mod.— No, Señor. The ladies were touched, and I heard them say, 'How good, how humble, how religious!'
Balt.— This is intolerable — intolerable! The very devil himself seems to be inspiring this man. The farce — the grand farce — the iniquity — the arch-iniquity is finished! There is no more! It is finished!

Scene VII

Don Baltasar, Don Modesto, Paco, and Angeles

Paco.— Is the wedding ceremony over?

Ang.— Yes, Señor; now they are married. (*Wiping her eyes.*)

Mod. (*kissing her on the forehead*).— My poor little girl! Just like me! You are touched, too. A wedding touches everybody.

Balt.— Well? Has nothing else happened?

Ang.— Yes, Señor, many things. How good Señor de Medina is! What a soul he has! What a heart! I don't say he's a saint, because they say there aren't any saints nowadays, but he is not like other men. I said so all the time, and they wouldn't believe me.

Balt.— I believe it.

Ang.— And all the ladies say so.

Balt.— What won't they say!

Mod.— Tell us, tell us. What has happened?

Ang.— You shall see. When everything was over — Oh, well, when they were married, Gabriel went up to the altar with a dignified and noble bearing, and, taking up a crucifix, went to where Fuensanta was, placed the crucifix on her heart, and said to her in a very gentle tone, 'Rejoice, Fuensanta, your God holds out his arms to you.' Fuensanta burst out crying, and all the rest of us did the same. How lovely! How tender!

Balt.— And the gentlemen?

Ang.— Oh, they are so hard-hearted, they didn't cry but they were touched too, I believe.

Balt.— And Señor de Torres?

Ang.— Who? The one they say is a doctor and a scholar? Ah! He glared at Gabriel with his eyes wide open, as if he wanted to eat him.

Balt.— Umph — umph!

Ang.— I believe he was envious of him.

Paco.— Scenes like this do not occur ordinarily; therefore I am inclined to believe that it is a very extraordinary scene.

Ang.— Right; it thrilled everybody. So much so that a gentleman — I don't know who he was, probably a newspaper reporter — took out a piece of paper and made a note.

Balt. (*joyfully*).— Ah! That was the notary! We shall see, we shall see; everything is not lost yet!

Mod.— And then? (*To his daughter.*)

Ang.— After that, nothing. A deluge of embraces and congratulations — all of us womenfolk crying, Fuensanta too — and — what more do you want?

Paco.— And Fuensanta?

Ang.— After so much emotion, the poor girl feels tired out — and everybody advises her to retire. Doña Andrea, Don Leandro, and Gabriel will do the honors to the guests.

Mod.— Fuensanta is coming?

Ang.— Right away; as soon as she bids them good night. Here she is now.

Scene VIII

Angeles, Don Baltasar, Don Modesto, Paco; *in the rear* Fuensanta, Doña Andrea; *the first and second ladies and the first and second gentlemen forming a group*

And.— So now shut yourself up all alone and get some rest.

First lady.— No wonder you broke down, poor child!

Second lady.— Good night, Fuensanta!

Ang.— Give me a hug and a kiss (*kissing her*), and good night.

Mod.— Let me congratulate you first. Good night, my child.

Fuen.— Thank you. Thank you. You are very kind.

Paco (*in a sad, affectionate tone, and with a solemn air*).— Whoever desires to see you happy, it is because he desires your happiness. Good night, Fuensanta! (*Giving her his hand.*)

Fuen. (*smiling*).— My most grateful thanks, Paquito.

Balt.— You know that I have always wished you well. Good intentions. I am somewhat brusque, but I am loyal. In times of trial — the same as ever — you will always find me at your side.

Fuen. (*looking at him steadily*).— I don't doubt it. Good night, Don Baltasar. (*All start away.* Fuensanta, *nervous and impatient, follows them with her gaze. Exeunt all.* Fuensanta *rings a bell, and a lackey and a maid appear.*) Lock these doors. (*The boy locks the three doors in the background.*) Turn out these lights; so much light annoys me. (*The maid turns out nearly all the electric lights.*) You may go. (*Remains alone.*)

Scene IX

Fuensanta, Gabriel, *as indicated by the dialogue*

Fuen.— Now I am alone! dear heaven, what a wearisome evening; What anxiety! How dear happiness costs! But at last I am happy! Now nobody has the right to torment me but Gabriel! This, this is all the happiness the world can give; to depend upon none but another being, whom one loves! Not to be answerable to the rest, as I have been during these two years. At last I am free — because at last I am a slave! What a happy woman I am! (*Pauses*) Happy — happy! Am I as happy as I say? Is there no drop of bitterness in the cup? No. What madness! How ungrateful to God! I don't know what is the cause of my agitation. I am afraid. Why should I fear? Those infamous creatures failed in their plots — they were seeking a scandal! and there was nothing of the kind. Gabriel's conduct was irreproachable. A mighty effort it cost him! When he went up to the altar and kissed it I trembled; when he laid the Crucifix on my breast I trembled. What a look he gives! Why did he look at me like that? His eyes were like two coals! Since then light scares me. It's very bright — very bright. (*Turns off the light; the stage remains in darkness, and she curls up in an armchair.*) It's better this way, but I am afraid to be in the dark, too. (GABRIEL *enters through one of the side doors.*) Who's that? Who's that? (*In fright.*)

Gab.— It is I. (*Walking slowly.*)

Fuen.— Ah! My Gabriel!

Gab.— Yes, your Gabriel!

Fuen.— But I can't see you; and I don't suppose you can see me. Shall I turn on the light?

Gab.— What for? I am seeking you, my Soul.

Fuen.— Good eyesight you have! (*Laughing.*) For I — nothing — nothing ——(*Pauses.*) Aren't you going to answer me? Where are you?

Gab. (*has seated himself on the oppostie side of the stage*).— Where should I be? Near my Fuensanta; very near.

Fuen.— Is that so? How queer! (*Extending her arms and groping for him.*) Why, I can't find you! No, you are fooling me! (*Fondly.*) You are far, far away!

Gab.— However far away I am I shall always be near you.

Fuen.— This shows your wisdom, Sir Scholar! (*Jokingly.*)

Gab.— So it does. (*Pauses.*)

Fuen.— Gabriel, are you still there?

Gab.— Yes, as always; I am always everywhere.

Fuen.— Why don't you come nearer? See how pleasant it is to be in the dark!

Gab.— We are doing very well as we are. Light is deceitful. Everybody thinks that the light is something very clear. Poor people! No; conscience is more luminous in the dark.

Fuen.— Just as you like, but it saddens me.

Gab.— No matter; you love earthly joys too well. They are false, traitorous, fleeting. Weep, weep, and you will be happy.

Fuen. (*rising and going toward him*).— Why do you say that? Are you angry with me?
Gab.— Angry with you? No, poor woman!
Fuen.— Don't call me ' poor woman'; call me ' Fuensanta.' In your letters you talked to me in quite another way. When you came you looked at me with love. This very night you sometimes roared with anger. You frightened me; but I preferred it all to this silence, this indifference; this supreme disdain which I feel in the shadow, falling out of the darkness and annihilating me. Say something! Answer! I thought you were very good; but no, you are not good! (*Fondly.*)
Gab.— Good is not an appropriate word; I am neither good nor evil; I am; I am.
Fuen.— No, for God's sake! Don't begin such things! You are — yes, you are! That is why I love you; not, however, because you are, but because you are my Gabriel! because you mistreat me, because you caress me! No! no! You are not caressing me! Your hands are cold. Your arms fall slack! something is the matter with you! I want to know it! You are hiding some secret from me!
Gab.— Ah! My secret! Yes! And I have come no farther than this! And I had already forgotten it! And I — groping — groping in the folds of the darkness! To what have I come? To what have I come? (*With great excitement.*) Yes, my life, my secret!
Fuen.— I knew it well! Exactly! Is it a sad secret? Perhaps a terrible secret!
Gab.— No; on the contrary, a secret all joy. Your sadness is over forever! A secret all light; when you know it, you will no longer ask for light, because you will have all the light of the universe upon your brow if only you place it near to mine!
Fuen.— This secret — how long have you known it?
Gab.— I have known it always. Yet I did not know it. It was within me, but so hidden that I did not know it! Look you! And I — though I am that I am — like every one else!
Fuen.— Like every one else?
Gab.— Yes, like every one else! One man more! At last I understood that I was not as all men! I felt within me an infinite power; so much as I wished I obtained. I felt within me an infinite intelligence; what I wished to know I knew; now I believe that I knew it before! I felt within me an infinite love. (*Pauses.*) Love for all! ' And why have I so great love? ' I asked myself. And often I said to myself when alone, ' For this reason: because you are '— but I pretended not to understand it! (*Laughs idiotically.*)

Fuen. (steps back in fright, pressing her head, disarranging her hair).— Gabriel! Gabriel! Wake up! Wake up!

Gab.— Yes, I said that to myself one day: 'Wake up!' and I waked up.

Fuen.— And what then? Finish it! I am going mad!

Gab.— And one day — listen, poor woman! one day I could bear it no longer. My heart leaped! My brain leaped! my being exploded within me! and all of me said to myself, 'But you are all! You are not Gabriel! You are ——

Fuen.— Who are you?

Gab.— Silence! I am ——

Fuen.— My Gabriel! (*With a despairing gesture.*)

Gab.— Not your Gabriel, no! That is a little thing! I am 'Your God!'

Fuen.— What! My God, yes, because Gabriel is my God! but nothing more than that! The God of Fuensanta, but nothing more! — No! No! (*Crazed with grief, raving, sobbing.*)

Gab.— No! Don't belittle me, woman! The God of all! The God of all! The one God, infinite, eternal! Do I not say God? Then God! Gabriel is God! I am He Who was, Who is, Who shall be!

Fuen.— Ah! No! Blessed Saviour! Hush! Hush! It's a lie! lie! lie!

Gab.— A lie — You say it is a lie! You deny me! Pride, cursed pride! (*In terrible accents; making her fall upon her knees.*)

Fuen. (on her knees, weeping).— Gabriel! Gabriel! No — it is a dream — a nightmare! My God! My God!

Gab.— At last you call upon me! So! Repent and weep! God is nourished by tears. (*In her ear. Pauses.* FUENSANTA *on the floor, weeping; he standing by her side.*)

SCENE X

FUENSANTA, GABRIEL; *by a side door* DON BALTASAR *and* a servant

Serv. (in a low tone).— Yes, Señor, yes — something is happening — as you told me to let you know.

Balt.— You have done right. You may go. (*Exit servant.*)

Fuen.— Oh, I have gone mad or I am dreaming! I must wake up! Wake me! Help! Help! Awake! Awake!

Gab.— Hush! hush! Your cries irritate me! If not, I will make you hush! Life is mine, silence is mine! (*Shaking her frantically.*)

Fuen.— Come to me! to me! Help! Salvation!

Balt. (*rushing between the two and separating them*).— Yes, Fuensanta, I will save you!

Gab.— Who are you?

Balt.— One who will know how to handle you. (*Seizing him by one arm.*)

Fuen.— No, not him! (*Trying to separate them.*)

Gab.— He, the wicked angel of darkness! Yes, let us fight! How beautiful to struggle in the darkness, to embrace the enveloping shadow, and feel oneself strong to conquer! (*They grapple in the dark;* GABRIEL *throws* BALTASAR. FUENSANTA, *as if mad, cries for help;* BALTASAR *utters cries of rage.* GABRIEL *laughs in frenzied joy.*)

LAST SCENE

FUENSANTA, GABRIEL, DON BALTASAR. *As the doors open in the background all the other characters of the drama appear, and a multitude of other ladies and gentlemen. The situation is as follows:* BALTASAR *senseless on the floor;* GABRIEL *victorious, almost trampling him down. The doors in the background open; the front in darkness, the salons in the rear brilliantly lighted, so as to make the contrast the greater. All the other persons huddled together at the doors, not yet fully cognizant of what is going on; at first glimpse they see no one but* GABRIEL *and* FUENSANTA. *Confused cries from all:* 'Madman!' 'He is mad!' 'He has lost his reason!' 'It was true!' 'He has killed him!' 'Save him!' 'It's Don Baltasar!' 'Catch him!' 'Catch him!' *They try to enter in a body and throw themselves upon* DON BALTASAR *and* GABRIEL, *but the latter advances fiercely upon them all and they fall back*

Est.— Madness!

Gab.— Back! Back! Do you know who I am?

Fuen.— No, Gabriel. Hush!

Gab.— Imbeciles! Do you know who I am?

Fuen.— Hush! Hush!

Gab.— Don't you know? Then you tell them! Tell it! (*To* FUENSANTA.) On your knees! And tell it — tell it, Fuensanta! (*Breaks into frenzied laughter; all rush forward; confusion, shouts, and laughter, and above all the cries of* FUENSANTA, *who shrieks*): Gabriel! Gabriel! Gabriel!

ACT IV

(SCENE: *The same as in Act II.* TIME: day)

SCENE I

RAMONA, RESTITUTO (servants)

Ram.— I tell you, Restituto, that it all looks mighty bad to me.

Rest.— Who are you talking to, Ramona? It's bad, is it? There's nothing to say about that.

Ram.— Were you in the salon the other night, the night of the wedding?

Rest.— I am always where my duty calls me.

Ram.— And you saw what happened?

Rest.— There's nothing to say about that; I saw what everybody saw.

Ram.— I was the one who let Don Baltasar know; he had told me to, because he was afraid of something.

Rest.— Well, when we opened the doors, and the ladies and gentlemen came in, we found Don Baltasar lying there like a log, like a dead man, and Don Gabriel trampling him. Oh, pshaw, that was too much.

Ram.— Just as they had said, ' Don Gabriel is mad, is mad!'

Rest.— There's nothing to say about that; Don Gabriel is crazier than a basketful of cats, even if that is a poor comparison.

Ram.— Poor Don Baltasar! It's true that he's a very bad character.

Rest.— There's nothing to say about that. As a bad character, he's got it. And look here; it didn't seem to us like a bad thing for Don Gabriel to give him a thrashing. When people are such wild beasts, it serves them right.

Ram.— Yes, but he came near killing him; for an officer has come in, and the poor gentleman has been very, very ill.

Rest.— He's been a little bit, and he's pretended a little more.

Ram.— Why, man, there's no reason to believe that!

Rest.— Believing is believing; we're not fools here, and we know pretty well where everybody's going.

Ram.— If Don Gabriel didn't have so much money, we know where he'd have gone — to jail. Just suppose you had been the one who had beaten Don Baltasar; and see where you'd be.

Rest.— There's nothing to say about that. But the Lord knows — the Lord knows ——

Ram.— What?

Rest.— That if they don't take him to jail, it's because they think they can take him somewhere else worse than that.

Ram.— Worse than jail?

Rest.— Because in jail there are sometimes people with sense, and in the place I'm talking about ——

Ram.— Ah! You mean?

Rest.— Well, then. It's plain that Don Gabriel is not right in his head.

Ram.— Exactly; that's he's lost his mind.

Rest.— And Don Paquito, with the talent that the Lord has given him for saying everything, said the other night, 'Gentlemen, from a man who has lost his reason, nothing reasonable is to be expected.'

Ram.— Well, you know, that's a fact.

Rest.— To be sure it is! Not a thing! Come, come! Don Paquito is Don Paquito!

Ram.— I've always believed that.

Rest.— There's nothing to say about that.

Ram.— Good; and what next?

Rest.— The others want to put Don Gabriel in a cage, you might say. What are cages for?

Ram.— For birds.

Rest.— And for people who are as they say poor Don Gabriel is.

Ram.— And the Señorita will consent to it?

Rest.— Well, even if she doesn't consent; because that is what the law is for — to make people do things that have to be done, whether they want to or not. I tell you, Don Gabriel is done up in paper. When you see a man done up in paper, you may say he's lost. I, for instance, am Restituto; everybody says to me, 'Restituto, Restituto,' and it's nothing; everything's all right; I eat and drink and sleep, and say that Ramona's a peach, and nothing happens. But they write 'Restituto' on a piece of stamped paper, and the notary marks a cross, and you may give me up for dead, for they've made my epithalamium!

Ram.— No, you're right; for a cousin of mine died in the presidio on account of signing a paper — poor fellow! But the Señorita has plenty of money.

Rest.— Well, even if she has, that means that she'll lose so much the more — her money and her husband, too. If they leave her her money, things won't be so bad.

Ram.— You don't know her.

Rest.— An angel of God, better than bread.

Ram.— An unchained lioness. She raves worse than the madman. What do you suppose she's thinking of doing?

Rest.— Do you know?

Ram.— I can imagine. Get into the lovely boat the Señorita has in the port, and go — to be swallowed up in the sea! The sea!

Rest. (laughing.)— Oh my! What a fine sight! The judge on the bank: ' I've got you in the paper! I've got you in the paper! ' Wet papers! And the notary on the shore, making crosses on the water. And the steamer belching smoke. Oh, but she's a smoker! And the engine goes: Puff, puff, puff, puff. Poor lady, they want to take her husband away! Because he's crazy! Well, suppose he is!

Ram.— The husbands that are not crazy don't seem any better.

Rest.— There's nothing to say about that; there are good ones and bad ones. But have you got any reason for what you say?

Ram.— I'll tell you.

Rest.— Tell away.

Ram.— Don Gabriel had two men come, two of those on the boat, two sailors; one is a Mexican, and the other, — I don't know whether he talks English; they say he's English. All right; well, he shut himself up in his office with them.

Rest.— The Señora too?

Ram.— The Señora wasn't there. Well, when they were leaving the two sailors were talking to each other; they said things I didn't understand, because they didn't talk plain, don't you know? When a man don't talk Spanish, you can't understand him. But the Mexican said: ' He orders it, and I'll do what he orders. I don't know what for, but he orders it.'

Rest.— And what were Don Gabriel's orders?

Ram.— I don't know. The one that talked English made an ugly face and shook his head.

Rest.— Well, I don't understand it.

Ram.— Nor I. But listen. Last night Don Gabriel got away and the Señora couldn't find him. We looked all over the house for him, without waking anybody, because the Señora didn't want to. Well, he went through the lower rooms with the two sailors; I didn't see them come in, but I did see them leave. All that gives you something to think about.

Rest.— Well, then, let's get to thinking, right away, because now I think the Señora is coming.

Ram.— Yes. Holy Mary! The Señora is mighty bad off! I believe she's going mad, the way they say the Señor is; and then the two of 'em ——

Rest.— Don Paquito has a saying: ' One madman makes a hundred.'
Ram.— Hush. (*The two retire to one side.*)

Scene II

Ramona, Restituto. Fuensanta, *right, nervous, pale, discomposed*

Fuen.— Nobody. Ah, you!
Ram.— Have you any orders, Señora?
Fuen.— Nothing. Go. No, wait. What time is it? (*Looking around for a clock.*)
Rest.— Five.
Fuen.— Five! Impossible; it must be later. What time does it turn dark?
Ram.— It's dark by seven.
Rest.— Black dark at eight.
Ram.— But there's a moon.
Fuen.— (*Angrily*).— What for? What for?
Rest.— Señora!
Fuen.— Yes. Very well. Don't say anything. I can't. I can't.
Ram.— Do you feel ill, Señora?
Fuen.— I? No. Leave me. (*They start to go.*) But don't go. (*Turns impetuously toward the rear of the gallery.*) Come here. (*To* Ramona *and* Restituto.) Do you see that yacht?
Ram.— That big boat? The houseboat?
Fuen.— Yes. Is the stack smoking?
Ram.— No, Señora.
Rest.— It seems to me that the stack is beginning to smoke.
Fuen.— Is that so? You have good eyes. It's true; I see something.
Ram.— That's clouds. No, Señora, they haven't fired up.
Fubn.— Why? Do you know it?
Ram.— I — no, Señora. But if the Señora or the Señor has ordered it ——
Fuen.— We have ordered nothing. And be careful how you go about telling lies!
Ram.— Señora, we ——
Fuen.— What time is it?
Rest.— A little after five.
Fuen.— That's what you said before! The same thing all the time! And Basilio?

Ram.— He went away a good while ago; he said that the Señora had ordered him to go after Don Leandro.

Fuen.— Has he come back?

Rest.— No, Señora.

Fuen.— When he does come back, have him come in at once.

Ram.— Yes, Señora.

Fuen.— But nobody else; he or Don Leandro. Do you understand?

Ram.— And if Doña Andrea comes, or Don Esteban?

Fuen.— I am receiving nobody, nobody.

Rest.— They sometimes insist — and we — we don't dare shut them out.

Fuen.— Whose orders are you taking?

Rest.— Señora, there's nothing to say about that.

Ram.— They shall be thrown out.

Fuen. (*running to the plate-glass in anguish*).— My God, my God, these hours! These hours! Hush! Is he calling me? Yes, it is he! it is he! I am coming, Gabriel. When I am dead, were that voice to call me — I must come! (*Exit, irresolute.*)

Scene III

Ramona, Restituto. *Afterwards,* Basilio

Ram.— Did you see how the poor Señora is?

Rest.— Oh, my, yes! It hurts you.

Ram.— It's the third time within two hours that she's gone out to see if they've fired up. What did I tell you?

Rest.— I believe you're right. Somebody's coming upstairs. (*Looking through the door in the rear.*) Here's Basilio.

Bas.— The Señora?

Ram.— In her rooms.

Bas.— Well, tell her I'm here.

Ram. (*with curiosity*).— Any news?

Rest. (*same way*).— Anything doing?

Bas.— No, nothing doing. Please tell her right away.

Ram.— Right away. (*Exit right, first wing.*)

Rest.— Do you know anything?

Bas.— No.

Rest.— Have you noticed anything?

Bas.— Yes; people that I don't like, policemen, too, around the house.

Rest.— Me, too. It's to keep him from getting away.

Bas.— Who?

Rest.— The master. Because the master is done up in paper.

Bas.— It's a disgrace to them all. Why? Let's see; why?

Rest.— Hush; here comes the mistress.

Scene IV

The same; Fuensanta, Romona, *right, first wing*

Fuen. (*seeing* Basilio).— Thank God!

Bas.— Señora ——

Fuen.— You may go. (*To* Ramona *and* Restituto. *The latter bow and retire, talking in a low tone.*)

Scene V

Fuensanta, Basilio

Fuen.— Did you find him?

Bas.— Yes, Señora.

Fuen.— And talked with him?

Bas.— Yes, Señora, I talked with Don Leandro.

Fuen.— In person?

Bas.— With Don Leandro in person.

Fuen.— And you told him ——

Bas.— That he is to come at once; at once; that the Señora is waiting for him with the greatest impatience.

Fuen.— And he will come?

Bas.— Right away. He ordered the carriage because he is not feeling well; and that's why he hasn't come before. But he'll come at once.

Fuen.— You've heard nothing? You've seen nobody? Really I'm depending upon you, because I know that you are good. Tell me what you know.

Bas.— I know nothing, Señora. But I have seen around the house people that I don't like.

Fuen.— I know now! They are watching us! We shall see, we shall see. Did you go to the yacht? Did you talk to the captain?

Bas.— I went there, too.

Fuen.— And they have not received Gabriel's orders? Then why don't they obey them? Why? Are they plotting to betray us? Why don't they fire up?

Bas.— They have begun to fire up; just now, when I came back, the stacks were beginning to smoke.

Fuen.— No, I tell you, no. No; come here! (*Taking him to the plate-glass.*) Look! Ah! Yes. At last. It was time!

Bas.— Do you see it, Señora? The two smokestacks, the two engines?

Fuen.— Yes, yes. Now they are beginning, but they will delay a long time — a long time! They say that it is a very slow process. Ah! What people! What people! What sluggishness! On our part, what sluggishness! On theirs — Don Baltasar, Don Esteban, all of them — what feverish activity!

Bas.— Don't worry, Señora; within an hour the boilers will be under pressure. Ah! Don Gabriel has brought on some A No. 1 machinists! Intelligent and daring! They'd just as soon throw a barrel of petroleum on the coal as not, to hurry things up! (*Laughing.*) They are devils of hell. And obedient and loyal! Bah! It's what Don Gabriel orders them, and nothing else! Be it what it may; even though it be an atrocity! He pays them well! Like slaves! Don't worry, Señora.

Fuen.— Ah, Basilio, you are giving me the food that I sorely need. And where shall we embark?

Bas.— On the park landing.

Fuen.— The launch has good oarsmen? Nobody can overtake us?

Bas.— Señora, it is a launch that flies! It has a petroleum engine!

Fuen.— Good! good! (*Looking through the plate-glass.*) I am consumed with impatience! Basilio, I am consumed! When will it be night?

Bas.— The sun sets in less than an hour.

Fuen.— How long a time yet! If I could only push the time forward! And bring many clouds and thick darkness! Look, wait outside in case I need you for anything.

Bas.— Yes, Señora.

Fuen.— Do you see? Do you see? Don Leandro's not coming!

Bas. (*looking at the door in the rear*).— Here he is, now!

Fuen.— Yes? Really? Ah! Yes! He! Go and wait outside here. (*Exit* BASILIO; *enter* DON LEANDRO.)

Scene VI

Fuensanta, Don Leandro

Fuen.— Ah, Don Leandro! I thought you were not coming!

Lean.— But, child, I really was coming; we said at six.

Fuen.— Yes. You are right! But I really can bear no more! I can bear no more!

Lean.— Come, Fuensanta, courage; courage, my child.
Fuen.— I have courage. You shall see!
Lean.— And you are continuing with your project?
Fuen.— With my project? But it is the only way, there is no other to defend ourselves against this infamy! Against these infamous creatures!
Lean.— Yes, that is true. But it involves a great risk. Have you thought it over deliberately? Alone with Gabriel? In his present condition?
Fuen.— What! You! You too! You've come to think as everybody does!
Lean.— No, I don't think as everybody else does. But one must not shut his eyes to the evidence.
Fuen. (in a distrustful tone).— What evidence?
Lean.— I don't want to grieve you, but Gabriel's condition - - —
Fuen.— What do you mean? Pronounce the horrible word! I am used to hearing it; he repeats it himself and laughs! Laughs! Come! You were the only one lacking! Gabriel is ——
Lean.— Well, then; if it is necessary I will pronounce it. Gabriel is——
Fuen.— Mad!
Lean.— I don't go so far.
Fuen.— Lie! Outrage! For the extravagance of a moment, for a natural excitement. Then all of us, all of us are mad; you, Don Baltasar, I myself — I more than anybody else. *(With rising excitement.)* I see everything in confusion; I can't co-ordinate two ideas; I hate everybody; and I'd like to strike, to destroy, so as to see — see what they would do with me.
Lean.— Gabriel came near killing Don Baltasar.
Fuen.— And I'd have done it, too, if I could; rest assured of that. That's not the point; that's not the point. Their plan is perfectly evident, and they are working it out: That Gabriel tried to kill Don Baltasar *(enumerating ironically)*; that everybody saw it; that it is public; very well. Is he in his right mind? Then to the jail, as a criminal. Has he lost his reason? Then to the madhouse. And meanwhile watch him. This, this is their project; I tell you, if you don't know. To take him away, separate him from me forever, forever, because such things never end. When, when is it certainly known that a man has or has not lost his reason! Months, years, the doubt lasts forever; and meanwhile, he will either really turn mad or else die of despair; and I shall die with him. And behind us we leave millions upon millions, shining silver, glittering, an immense fortune, a mountain of treasures, and human avarice centered upon them. Don

Baltasar, with his hooked talons; Don Esteban, with his glittering eyes; Paquito, with his idiot laugh; Don Modesto, slobbering like a dog; Andrea, with her tremulous mouth; all satiating themselves; and Gabriel and Fuensanta rotting in the ground with less pain than these miserable creatures feel in their consciences.

Lean.— You are right; all that is true; but what is to be done to obviate it, when fate ties our hands? The strength is theirs, the law is with them; they are looking out for their interests, but they are defending the truth.

Fuen.— The truth? And you say so?

Lean.— Yes; there is no use deceiving yourself. Gabriel has lost his reason!

Fuen.— Ah! You believe it? You believe it in good faith?

Lean.— And you, too; though with sublime obstinacy you force yourself not to admit it to any one, even to yourself, and you shut your eyes so as not to see, your ears so as not to hear; and you cling to Gabriel in despair. I admire you, but I can do nothing more,— the evidence overwhelms me.

Fuen.— Well, not me; first, because it is not evidence, but error and evil; and in any case because I do not need to convince myself of anything to do what I must.

Lean.— And what is that?

Fuen.— You know it already, flee; it is in your power to betray us.

Lean.— Fuensanta! (*Protesting indignantly.*)

Fuen.— Yes, flee; in a little while, as soon as night falls; to the yacht and freedom! Do they want to bar our passage? So much the worse for those who try it. The crew disembark — abandoned people, soulless people — what you will; I say sublime people, who obey Gabriel as God; and they will open the way for us with bullets.

Lean.— Fuensanta, my child, but you are raving! GABRIEL *has appeared in the background; he now has the unmistakable aspect of a madman. And slowly, cautiously, looking distrustfully around, he slips along in the rear until he reaches the door of the staircase. It makes a noise in opening and* FUENSANTA *and* DON LEANDRO *turn; he stops and shrinks like a child caught in mischief.*)

SCENE VII

FUENSANTA, GABRIEL, DON LEANDRO

Fuen.— Ah, Gabriel!
Lean.— Gabriel!

Gab.— I wasn't going to do anything wrong; I wasn't going to escape. (*Preparing to go back, and speaking with fear and shrinking.*)
Lean.— You see, my child?
Gab.— Very well, then, I'll go back. I'll go back to my room. You needn't be vexed.
Fuen.— No, Gabriel, come here and let's talk seriously.
Gab. (*coming forward*).— Seriously! But there is nothing serious in this world, nothing that's worth being serious about, is there?
Fuen.— You see!
Gab.— Yes, the world is an eternal masquerade. Nothing disguised itself as nothing, and everything was without form and void; the infinite germ of creation. Then crack: I gave it a thump, the great mask fell, and space precipitated no end of suns and worlds.
Lean.— You see, poor Fuensanta! And you did this? For you — we know what you are. (*To* GABRIEL.)
Gab.— Silence, this is not to be talked about, not to be published, for imagine: I say ' I am God,' and the others say that I am mad. Then, if God has lost His senses, think what is to become of the universe! (*With a strident laugh.*) Unhappy creatures! Unhappy creatures!
Lean.— Unhappy you, unhappy this poor woman! (GABRIEL *walks back and forth, talking to himself, smiling and looking maliciously at the others.*)
Fuen.— Stop and think — we must defend ourselves.
Gab.— Who?
Fuen.— We.
Gab.— Against whom?
Fuen.— Against them — against those who covet my fortune — against those who are trying to separate us.
Gab. (*embracing her*).— Separate us! Let them try it!
Fuen.— You won't allow it, really?
Gab.— Let them try it!
Fuen.— In that case we shall have to flee!
Gab.— Ah, yes, your idea! (*Smiling.*) Poor little girl! What have you to think of? (*Condescendingly.*) For I have things arranged already. That's what I came here for. Call him — him. You understand? I don't know his name — no matter.
Fuen.— Basilio?
Gab.— Very well, it may be Basilio, — just as it may be anybody else whatsoever.

Fuen.— He is the most trustworthy. (Fuensanta *approaches the door of the background and calls him.*) Basilio! Basilio!
Bas. (*entering*).— Señora!
Fuen.— The Señor is calling you, come, quick!

Scene VIII

Fuensanta, Gabriel, Don Leandro, *and* Basilio

Bas. (*approaching* Gabriel).— Señor.
Gab.— What do you want?
Fuen.— To obey your orders; he is very faithful, he loves us dearly; he would throw himself into the fire for us. (Gabriel *bursts out laughing.*)
Gab.— You — you would be capable. Now I remember. (*To* Don Leandro.) You said I did not remember. He is good (*in a low tone to* Fuensanta *in reference to* Don Leandro), but very weak minded.
Fuen.— Gabriel!
Gab. (*taking a paper out of his pocket*).— Come here and listen. (*To* Basilio, *solemnly.*) Go, take this to the yacht. You know? Look, that boat (*taking him to the plate-glass*), the one that's smoking. Beautiful, isn't it? Men have made beautiful things! No, once in a while they are not so stupid as I said. Ordinarily they are very stupid, very idiotic, but they have sparks of genius. I know why! (*Maliciously.*)
Fuen.— Gabriel, you are letting your mind wander!
Gab.— Yes, I frequently let my mind wander, and the world gets into a fine plight when I grow absent-minded! (Don Leandro *makes a movement;* Fuensanta *anticipates him.*)
Fuen.— Come. (*Tenderly, but with determined purpose to defend him.*)
Gab.— Well, go, take this paper to that beautiful boat; to mine. That is to say, all of them are mine; everything is mine; but, in a word, the one you call mine. You understand? (*Extending his hand as if to clasp space, giving the paper to* Basilio.)
Bas.— Yes, Señor; I will give this letter to the captain.
Gab.— No, not to the captain; to one of those men who came here yesterday. Do you know them?
Bas.— Yes, Señor. Two sailors with very bad faces.
Gab. (*looking at him and smiling*).— They are the ones. Go quick! (*Exit* Basilio, *rear.*)
Fuen.— You are giving them orders to be ready to come for us? (*To* Gabriel.)

Gab. (absent-mindedly).— Yes, exactly. Bad faces! He says they have bad faces!

Fuen.— They are very rough, he meant.

Gab.— No, bad faces. Well, all men have bad faces. The first day of creation they were not so; to-day they are. (*Walking pensively to and fro.*) That primitive beauty has become extinct! To-day they are monstrous, ridiculous, ugly!

Fuen.— Gabriel!

Gab.— Be silent, listen, and learn. You don't know in what the difference consists? I shall explain it to you. (*Calls them to him; places himself between the two.*) It is the soul! Do you take that in? eh? It is the soul! Picture to yourselves a pasteboard puppet, which has a steel axis to keep it straight. So long as the axis is straight, the puppet, in spite of the inferior character of the material it is made of, is straight, well shaped, almost graceful. But the axis becomes bent, and the puppet with it; along with the axis it becomes twisted and distorted and humped. Well, the axis of the human body is the soul! Alas, if the soul becomes bent! The blemishes, the defects, the wrinkles, the deformities of the body are the blemishes, defects, wrinkles, deformities of the soul! Ah, you pasteboard puppet, before becoming outwardly deformed, you had to become deformed within! (*Raging, panting.*)

Fuen.— All this is the truth! Because he says these things, there is no reason to say he is mad. (*To* Don Leandro, *who hangs his head sadly. Pauses.*)

Lean.— And you are going to rectify all this?

Gab.— Certainly.

Lean.— How?

Gab.— Everything must be purified!

Lean.— In what way?

Gab.— I cannot say; you would be frightened. Above all, my poor Fuensanta; she does not need it, but she must sacrifice herself for the rest, as I do. Not you, because you are a good gentleman, but it will be hard to be sacrificed for oneself (*smiling benevolently*).

Lean.— Fuensanta! (*In a low tone.*)

Fuen.— I will hear nothing! He is a sage, a saint, if he is not God, he is my God. That is enough! (*Moving away from* Don Leandro. Gabriel *walks to and fro, absent-minded, talking to himself.*)

Scene IX

FUENSANTA, GABRIEL, DON LEANDRO, RESTITUTO

Rest.— Señora!

Fuen.— What?

Rest.— Don Esteban, Doña Andrea, and her son have come, and they say that they wish to see you.

Fuen.— And did you not tell them?

Rest.— Yes, Señora, but they insist that it is urgent, that it is necessary, that it is very important.

Fuen.— No, no. I won't see them; let them go away!

Lean.— Perhaps that is not prudent.

Fuen.— It may be. Then you go, see what they want,— gain time.

Lean.— Yes; I'll go. (*Returns, approaches* FUENSANTA *affectionately, with emotion.*) You distrust me?

Fuen.— No! Forgive me! I don't know what I am saying! I am going to lose my senses and I am going to lose my mind! For God's sake, hurry!

Lean.— Yes, courage! I don't know. I don't know. I don't know what I ought to do. (*Exit, rear, with* RESTITUTO.)

Scene X

FUENSANTA *and* GABRIEL. *Twilight; the sky, as seen through the plate-glass, filling with rosy clouds*

Fuen.— Gabriel. (GABRIEL *is looking at the sky.*)

Gab.— Ah, is it you? (*As if awaking from a dream.*) Look, the sun is setting; his last rays are touching this mass of clouds with flame; it looks like an immense conflagration on the sea! Beautiful, beautiful! Everything is exquisite!

Fuen.— Gabriel, you frighten me!

Gab.— That is but natural!

Fuen.— If they should hear you, they would say, if they should hear you, you would be lost! Only a God can say these things; if a man says them he is undone, he is forever undone! (*With horror.*)

Gab.— True! You speak well; if a man says them, to the madhouse, to the cell, to the straitjacket — as being imbecile, arrogant, sacrilegious. I would not brook it!

Fuen.— Gabriel! Gabriel, how you frighten me, how you horrify me! See, I have been struggling for days with an idea, a black idea! It is the contagion, the accursed contagion! Yes, they have infected me. Repeating to myself by day and by night in a whisper. ' Gabriel is!—Gabriel is!—Gabriel is!'—No, no. I must not finish it, I must not think it, I must not say it. (*Flinging herself upon him, seizing hold of his hands and clasping them about her neck.*) Strangle me, Gabriel! If you are a man, kill me; if you are God, kill me too! Death and oblivion and silence, for you, for me, for God! (*Swoons and falls into* GABRIEL'S *arms.*)

Gab. (*clasping his hands about her neck and caressing her.*)— How beautiful you are, how good, and how perfectly you weep! How gentle your eyes; how melodious your voice; between your sobs how round and how smooth your neck!

Fuen.— So — so — then speak to me so! That suffices for me!

Gab.— True; in telling you I love you, I have told you all.

Fuen. (*with infinite sweetness; something of earthly passion*).— Do you see? When you speak thus, my Gabriel, I understand you; and nobody will dare to say ——(*Checking herself.*)

Gab.— What?

Fuen.— Nothing. What matters it to us what the world says?

Gab.— To me, nothing. It is enough for me to hear your voice; it is so sweet. Go on. Go on. Always to hear you! Even though you repeat the same thing over and over, it matters not.

Fuen.— Why did you say those fantastic things before? Why?

Gab.— I don't know. Why, what did I say?

Fuen.— Oh, you know. It was to test me; wasn't it? It was to see whether I was like all of them, whether I would deny my Gabriel, wasn't it?

Gab.— Deny! Ah! It would not be the first time they have denied me. (*With a mysterious air.*) Thrice! Thrice!

Fuen. (*covering his mouth*).— No; hush! You are going to torment me again!

Gab.— No, not to torment you. I want you to be very happy.

Fuen.— Yes, both of us to be very happy. See, the night is coming. We two alone to the yacht — to the sea! And here they stay, writhing with anger! Come! Come!

Gab.— Writhing with anger — and we happy.

Fuen.— Yes.

Gab. (*pensively*).— Wait! An idea occurs to me, a doubt assails me. For us liberty, love — and he — he — there is a poor creature ——

Fuen.— Who?

Gab.— Yes; he deserves condemnation and punishment, but he is so unfortunate! And upon me depends his not being so. (*Pensively.*)

Fuen.— But who?

Gab.— He who fell! He who suffers! Satan!

Fuen.— Ah! Again, again; Jesu! Jesu! No, hush! I won't listen, I won't listen! You, my Gabriel, an intelligence so noble, a heart so beautiful, you, to have lost your reason! Not to be yourself! To be, I don't know what — a machine to repeat sonorous phrases, the grotesque phantasm of what you were! Gabriel! Gabriel! To hold in your arms a being you love and not to have him! To look for his eyes and find nothing but flashes of fire, as if something were burning within! Awake from the dead! My soul, come — come — come to me!

Gab.— You will not reverence your God, wretched creature! (*Shakes her and almost throws her down.*)

Fuen.— Gabriel! Oh, Gabriel! If anything of Gabriel remains in you, have compassion on Fuensanta! (*Falls almost senseless, weeping, writhing, sobbing despairingly.*)

Gab.— Poor woman! poor woman, she does not understand me! (*Walks to and fro, looking at her from time to time.*)

Scene XI

The same, and Don Leandro *headlong from the rear*

Lean.— Fuensanta!

Fuen.— What? (*Raising her head.*)

Lean.— Courage! They are all coming, they are going to take him away.

Fuen.— Him! No! (*Rises to her feet with a new accession of energy.*)

Lean.— They wish to come in.

Fuen.— I forbid it.

Lean.— They have a warrant from the judge.

Fuen.— I forbid it.

Lean.— See, they are coming up.

Fuen. (*rushing to the door*).— Yes. Ah, Gabriel, come in here, I beg of you!

Gab.— What for?

Fuen.— To defend yourself. I beseech you. (*Pulling him toward the right.*)

Gab.— Alone!

Fuen.— You are never alone. I am with you, always.

Gab.— That is true. I am never alone. (*Laughing.*) A good lesson! A lesson to your God. Thank you, thank you, a thousand times! (*Exit.*)
Fuen. (*smoothing her disordered hair, readjusting her clothing, placing herself before the door in a tragic attitude*).— To defend him! I will not leave him! Is he my God? Then with my God! Is he a poor madman? With my madman! They shall not separate us! The rotten and miserable reality of their selfishness is coming to the assault against the sublime madness of our love! Let them come! I am waiting for them!

Scene XII

Fuensanta, Don Leandro, Don Esteban, Doña Andrea, Paco, *enter from the rear.* Fuensanta *always before the door through which* Gabriel *has gone out, covering it with her body*

And.— Fuensanta! (*All advance.* Fuensanta *stops them with a gesture.*)
Fuen.— Did you wish to see me? (*To* Andrea.) Did you wish to see me? (*To the rest.*)
Est.— Yes, we did.
Fuen.— Well, here I am.
And.— And Gabriel?
Fuen.— Well. Perfectly well, as usual. (*Feigning naturalness and indifference.*)
Est.— I admire you, Fuensanta, I admire you! You surely know what is going on.
And.— Courage!
Est.— Courage, Fuensanta!
Fuen.— What a solemn tone! Some danger is threatening Gabriel and me; is that it?
Est.— No, not a danger. Your welfare is at stake, and at most there is no need to exaggerate the facts. Don Baltasar has suffered a terrible assault — he has been at the point of death. (Fuensanta *makes a disdainful gesture.*) So the doctors say. If Gabriel can present himself in public, if he is in possession of his reason, there will be nothing more to it. We have anticipated ourselves, and the conflict will be easily settled.
Fuen.— But to the point. What do you want?
Est.— We? To tell you — to give you notice that Don Baltasar coming — that he brings an order from the judge.

Fuen.— And men to enforce it.

Est.— For Gabriel to appear.

Fuen.— No.

Est.— It will be necessary. He must obey.

Fuen.— I will not; nor Gabriel either.

Est.— If Gabriel is well, what difference does it make? Ah! If he should give signs of — of mental aberration then he would be placed under surveillence for several days.

Fuen.— This — this is your pretence. Infamous conspiracy!

And.— For heaven's sake, Fuensanta! (*All protest.*)

Fuen.— Even if it were so, which it is not, but even if it were so, what business is it of anybody else? If he is mine, if I wish to keep him with me, who has the right to interfere?

Est.— Yes, child, the judge has that right; in the case you suppose, he would be a violent madman, because he tried to kill Don Baltasar, and precautions must be taken; he must be put into a safe place for your own sake. Your life is in danger.

Fuen.— But my life is my own! Suppose I do want to sacrifice it!

Est.— In this way you cannot. (*They surround her, with solicitude.*)

Fuen. (*in anguish, losing her self-control.*) But he is well, I tell you. He is well! Say so, Don Leandro! You have seen him!

Lean.— I? Yes, it is true, he is as usual. (*All say at the same time,* Let him show himself! ')

Est.— Well, then, let him show himself!

And.— Certainly, let him show himself!

Fuen.— No — I understand it all, and I will not give him up! Gabriel is in his right mind, but I will not yield to the infamous conspiracy! And now you — out — out — I will not see you! (*Advances fiercely upon them; they fall back.*)

Scene XIII

Fuensanta, Doña Andrea, Don Leandro, Don Esteban, Paco, Don Modesto, Don Baltasar; *in the rear, outside, but plainly visible, two sinister men, a cross between madhouse attendants and constables; indefinite in character, so to speak, but fear-inspiring.*

Balt.— No, Fuensanta, it must be carried through.

Fuen.— You lied, you lied, and these, these! Who are these? Oh, my head! Oh, my Gabriel! Don Leandro, for God's sake — for God's sake!

Lean.— Yes, my child!

Balt.— It grieves me sadly, sadly!

Fuen.— Hypocrite! Villain! Villain!

Balt.— I forgive you; you don't know what you are saying! I come, not to satiate a thirst for vengeance, I come not to impose a punishment. This unfortunate did not know what he was doing, but to clear this matter up and save you. I come resolved to save you.

Fuen.— To save me! You! Who are you? I can't find words — I can't find them.

Balt.— Give Gabriel up to us. I assure you that he shall be treated kindly — as what he is.

Fuen.— I have said no — and I have said no! And no one shall pass this door!

Balt.— Don't compel me to use force. (*The two men in the rear advance.*)

Fuen.— No, not that! Not those men! Pardon! Pardon! I will humble myself! I will humble myself! My God! My God! I cannot stand against all! Ah! (*With new and sudden resolution.*) Well, then, what help is there for it? I give up, as I have the assurance that he will put you to confusion, I submit. (*Triumphant joy among all.*) I am going myself to bring him, to surrender him to you as Judas surrendered Christ. Yes, I am going. (*Takes a few steps; her strength fails, and she falls upon the sofa.*) I cannot! (*They try to come to her, but she repulses them. Aside.*) No, no, I could not. I would be a hindrance to Gabriel! Don Leandro, you go please, and bring him. (*Embracing him; in a low tone.*) Tell him to fly by the inner door, I am coming after him. Do you understand? Have him come!

Lean.— Yes, I understand; yes! We shall save him! (*Exit, right, first wing.*)

Scene XIV

Fuensanta, Doña Andrea, Don Baltasar, Don Esteban, Don Modesto, *and* Paco

Fuen.— And while he is coming — listen to me — I have still something to tell you. They draw near with curiosity. And now I am going to tell you what I think! Don't interrupt me. (*Protesting.*) I read in the depths of your consciences — Consciences! let us drop this name. I love Gabriel; you want my money; for me, my love; for you, your gold, that is to say, mine; let us strike the bargain.

Balt.— This cannot be listened to. ('No, no, impossible,' *all exclaim in protest.*)

Fuen.— True, it cannot be listened to, but it can be thought about; let us compromise! I am going to die; very soon. Don't feign sadness, because I don't believe you. Very well; I will make a will in your favor, and you leave me Gabriel. (*Grand movement of protest, but of a different sort from the first.*)

Balt.— For heaven's sake! for heaven's sake!

Est.— Child, hush!

Fuen.— And on the spot — millions — millions — Two, four, ten, twenty!

Balt.— No more! No more! (*Protests follow.*)

Est. (*aside to* Paco).— How many did she say?

Paco.— She said four!

Mod.— No, ten; no, twenty!

Scene XV

The same, Don Leandro, *very much agitated*

Lean.— He is not there, he is not there, he has fled! the doors are locked on the outside!

Fuen.— Ah! At last! He is not there — he is not there! — You have lost your prey!

Balt.— He is not here? He has fled.

Lean. (*to* Fuensanta).— He was not there. I didn't find him!

Fuen.— Run, for God's sake, look for him, have him embark!

Lean.— Yes. (*Exit, rear.*)

Est.— The yacht is still there (*peering through the plate-glass*), we can catch him!

All.— Yes, yes, catch him. (*They rush toward the rear, talking, gesticulating with the vehemence of wild beasts.*)

Last Scene
All; a little later, Gabriel, *from the rear; now unmistakably mad; his dress and his aspect in wild disorder; uttering shrieks of laughter*

Fuen. (*crossing through the whole throng; rushing to the door in the rear, covering it with her body, mad, desperate*).— No! You shall not pass! You shall not pass! I am defending this door! Back! back! I give you everything, everything; riches — millions — gold — as much as you want — my blood, my life, my last breath — but you shall not pass!

Balt.— Fuensanta, don't force us — get away!

And.— We beseech you!

Fuen.— Force, then; dead, if you will, but not alive! Back! Back!

Balt.— Force, then. (*All advance upon her.*)

Fuen.— I can do no more. My God!

Gab. (*appears at this moment and catches her in his arms as she is about to fall.*)— Fuensanta!

Fuen.— Gabriel, ah, Gabriel! (*Falls into his arms almost senseless.*)

Gab.— Back! Back! I am I! I! (*All recede;* GABRIEL *and* FUENSANTA *in the center; the sinister men, madhouse keepers, constables, or whatever they are, in the rear with stupid and curious faces; the other characters in a confused mass in front.*) Ah! Now you have me, now you have found me; every one finds me — he who seeks me and he who seeks me not! Now we are all here! All together! Joy! (*With laughter and shouts of glee.*) Alleluia! Alleluia! Hosanna! Hosanna!

Balt. (*to the sinister men*).— Take hold of him; the attack of madness is beginning.

Est.— Yes, he is going to strangle Fuensanta in his arms. (*All advance upon him, the sinister men included; seeing his attitude, his look, his aspect, they recede.*)

Gab.— To me, come to me. Your hour has come — my hour has come! (*Behind the plate-glass appears a ruddy glow, as also in the stairway in the rear, and the door which leads to it. The conflagration is beginning.*)

Balt.— What is that — that glow?

And.— Flames!

Est.— Fire! (*Horrible scene of confusion;* GABRIEL *in the center, immovable, pressing* FUENSANTA, *who has fainted, to his breast. All shout, turn round and round, like the damned, run hither and thither; disjointed phrases, desperation, etc. Accusations, threats; these words are confusedly heard.*)

And.— Help — Help!

Balt.— The door, no, this way!

And.— Son!

Est.— Damnation, make way! Ah

Balt.— Miserable — the flames!

Est.— The flames,— they are rising, they are coming in!

And.— My God — mercy!

Est.— Damned! (*All the characters like mad.*)

Gab. (*amid the cries and the confusion, the growing conflagration and the entering flames, impassive, immovable, embracing* FUENSANTA *and mingling his shouts and his laughter with the shrieks of the rest.*) Yes! Damned! Damned! The hour has come — punishment — purification! Did you say madman? Then madman — your God — the madman divine! Gabriel is not Gabriel, he is the madman divine — the madman divine! (*He and Fuensanta stand apparently enveloped in flames.*)

www.ingramcontent.com/pod-product-compliance
Lightning Source LLC
Chambersburg PA
CBHW032022040426
42448CB00006B/703